NINE-PATCH
Extravaganza

By Judy L. Laquidara

American Quilter's Society
P.O. Box 3290 • Paducah, KY 42002-3290
FAX: 270-898-1173   www.AmericanQuilter.com

RECEIVED FEB

D1088447

746.46041 Laq

Laquidara, J.
Nine-patch extravaganza.

PRICE: $18.53 (3797/an   )

Located in Paducah, Kentucky, the American Quilter's Society (AQS) is dedicated to promoting the accomplishments of today's quilters. Through its publications and events, AQS strives to honor today's quiltmakers and their work and to inspire future creativity and innovation in quiltmaking.

Editor: Linda Baxter Lasco
Graphic Design: Mary Beth Head
Cover Design: Michael Buckingham
Photography: Charles R. Lynch

Library of Congress Cataloging-in-Publication Data

Laquidara, Judy L.
  Nine-patch extravaganza / by Judy L. Laquidara.
    p. cm.
  Summary: "Twelve full-sized quilt projects featuring the classic nine-patch block. A variety of techniques are used to give a fresh look to the simple nine-patch. Clear and concise cutting instructions and easy construction techniques for quilters of all levels of experience"–Provided by publisher.
  ISBN 978-1-57432-933-9
  1. Patchwork–Patterns. 2. Quilting–Patterns. I. Title. II. Title: 9-patch extravaganza.
  TT835.L354 2007
  746.46'041–dc22

                              2007014209

Additional copies of this book may be ordered from the American Quilter's Society, PO Box 3290, Paducah, KY 42002-3290; 800-626-5420 (orders only please); or online at www.AmericanQuilter.com. For all other inquiries, call 270-898-7903.

Copyright © 2007, Author, Judy L. Laquidara

All rights reserved. No part of this book may be reproduced, stored in any retrieval system, or transmitted in any form, or by any means including but not limited to electronic, mechanical, photocopy, recording, or otherwise, without the written consent of the author or publisher. Patterns may be copied for personal use only.

Proudly printed and bound in the United States of America.

ACKNOWLEDGMENTS

A special thanks to my husband, Vince, and my son, Chad, who have been so kind and understanding as I've gone through the process of writing the patterns and making the quilts for this book.

My quilting friends Vicky McGee and Becky Krampe have been a constant source of enthusiasm, encouragement, and help. Thanks for being there for me when I needed a boost.

To Betty Cummings at the Village Mercantile in Boonville, Indiana, thank you for your patience and advice as I chose fabrics for the quilts in this book.

Thanks to my mom, JoNell Miller, for the opportunity to play on that little black Singer® Featherweight on the kitchen table when I was about 10 years old. I fell in love with fabric and sewing and that love continues.

My most heartfelt thanks to Bonnie Browning, Barbara Smith, Linda Baxter Lasco, and the staff at the American Quilter's Society. You believed in me, you have answered my questions, and have always made me feel like a real author!

TABLE OF CONTENTS

PROJECTS

INTRODUCTION

Quilters have been using the simple Nine-Patch block in their quilts for years. The basic block is made of three rows, each consisting of three squares. Variations of the Nine-Patch block provide limitless possibilities for quilt designs. There are equal Nine-Patch blocks, which are typical of those we most often recognize as Nine-Patches, but there are also unequal Nine-Patch blocks, which offer a lot more variety. In Barbara Brackman's book *Encyclopedia of Pieced Quilt Patterns*, there are hundreds of blocks of both types.

For years, I have told my quilting friends that I never make anything harder than a Nine-Patch. With just a few exceptions, all of the quilts I have made include some variation of the Nine-Patch block. Any time I can disguise a block or set it so that the block blends into a whole quilt and doesn't appear to be single blocks set together, I feel that I have created a successful quilt design.

In this book you will find 12 patterns made from Nine-Patch variations. By using pieced sashing, rotating portions of blocks, coloring portions of blocks differently, or setting Nine-Patches with alternating blocks, many beautiful quilt designs can be created.

The Magic
of Nine-Patch

Simple construction...

...Spellbinding results!

Old COUNTRY Stars

Quilt size: 68" x 84"
Finished block size: 12" x 12"

The sashing gives the stars the appearance of floating and, better yet, results in no points to match! The checkerboard border is also quick, and it frames the quilt nicely.

Made and quilted by the author.

FABRIC REQUIREMENTS

Taupe	☆	$4^{1}/_{8}$ yards
Red Print	★	2 yards
Dark Olive Print	★	$^{5}/_{8}$ yard
Light Olive Print	★	$^{5}/_{8}$ yard
Binding	★	$^{3}/_{4}$ yard
Backing	★	$5^{3}/_{8}$ yard
Batting	★	76" × 90"

CUTTING INSTRUCTIONS
Use fabric at least 40" wide.

☆ Taupe   *Cut into:*

6 strips	$4^{1}/_{2}$" wide	48 A
11 strips	$2^{1}/_{2}$" wide	48 B, 8 strips for checkerboard border
2 strips	$5^{1}/_{4}$" wide	12 C
11 strips	$3^{1}/_{2}$" wide	6 G, 10 strips for border 1 sides and border 3
12 strips	$1^{1}/_{4}$" wide	34 F
3 strips	$1^{1}/_{2}$" wide	(pieced sashing)
3 strips	4" wide	(border 1 top & bottom)

★ Red Print

1 strip	$4^{1}/_{2}$" wide	4 A
1 strip	$5^{1}/_{4}$" wide	4 C
1 strip	$4^{7}/_{8}$" wide	8 D
1 strip	$2^{3}/_{4}$" wide	(pieced sashing)
8 strips	$2^{1}/_{2}$" wide	(checkerboard border)
8 strips	$3^{1}/_{2}$" wide	(border 4)

★ Dark Olive Print

1 strip	$4^{1}/_{2}$" wide	4 A
1 strip	$5^{1}/_{4}$" wide	4 C
1 strip	$4^{7}/_{8}$" wide	8 D
2 strips	$2^{3}/_{4}$" wide	9 E, 1 strip for pieced sashing

★ Light Olive Print

1 strip	$4^{1}/_{2}$" wide	4 A
1 strip	$5^{1}/_{4}$" wide	4 C
1 strip	$4^{7}/_{8}$" wide	8 D
2 strips	$2^{3}/_{4}$" wide	8 E, 1 strip for pieced sashing

★ Binding	9 strips $2^{1}/_{2}$" wide
★ Backing	2 panels 38 " × 92"
★ Batting	76" × 92"

A
$4^{1}/_{2}$" × $4^{1}/_{2}$" square

B
$2^{1}/_{2}$" × $2^{1}/_{2}$" square

C
$5^{1}/_{4}$" × $5^{1}/_{4}$" square

D
$4^{7}/_{8}$" × $4^{7}/_{8}$" square

E
2" × $2^{3}/_{4}$" rectangle

F
$1^{1}/_{4}$" × $12^{1}/_{2}$" rectangle

G
$3^{1}/_{2}$" × $3^{1}/_{2}$" square

CONSTRUCTION TECHNIQUES

Partial Quarter-Square Triangles (page 89)
Corner-Squares (page 90)
Border Application (page 91)

BLOCK CONSTRUCTION

Make 48 partial quarter-square triangles as shown in figure 1.

Figure 1

Make 16   Make 16   Make 16

Using the corner-square method, add four taupe B squares to each of the four print A squares to make 12 square-in-a-square units (figure 2).

Figure 2

Make 4   Make 4   Make 4

Referring to figure 3, assemble the blocks.

Figure 3

Block 1   Block 2   Block 3
Make 4   Make 4   Make 4

SASHING CONSTRUCTION

Make a strip-set with a 2¾" print strip and a 1½" taupe strip (figure 4). Make two more strip-sets like this, but each with a different print. Cut 2" segments from the three strip-sets for a total of 51 segments.

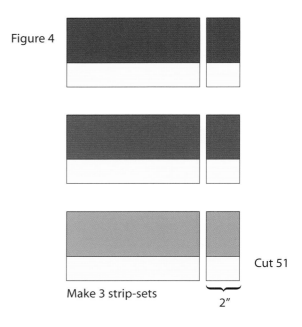

Figure 4

Cut 51

Make 3 strip-sets   2"

Join three segments plus an E rectangle of dark or light olive in a random arrangement for the sashing (see figure 5). Make 17 segment strips like this.

Add a taupe F rectangle to both sides of the segment strips to create the sashing units (figure 5).

Figure 5

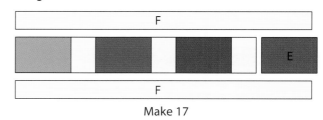

Make 17

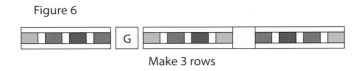

Referring to figure 6, make three sashing rows with 9 sashing units and taupe G squares.

Figure 6

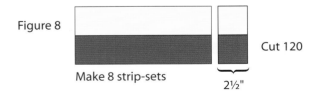

Make 3 rows

QUILT TOP ASSEMBLY

Arrange the Star blocks, then add the remaining 8 sashing units to make the block rows (figure 7).

Figure 7

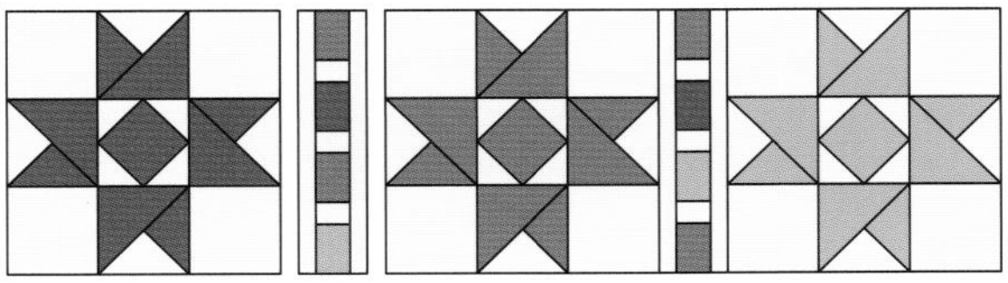

Make 4 rows

Join the block and sashing rows (see figure 11, page 12).

For taupe border 1, add the 3½" strips to the sides of the quilt, then add the 4" strips to the top and bottom (see figure 11, page 12).

The top needs to measure 48½" x 64½", including seam allowances, for the next border to fit.

For the checkerboard border, make eight strip-sets, each with a taupe 2½" strip and a red 2½" strip. Cut 120 segments 2½" (figure 8).

Figure 8

Cut 120

Make 8 strip-sets

2½"

Sew two segments together to make 60 four-patch units (figure 9).

Figure 9

Make 60

The four-patch units are turned differently for the side borders than for the top and bottom borders. Pay close attention to figure 10.

Join 16 four-patch units for each side border and add them to the quilt. Join 14 four-patch units for the top and bottom borders and add them to the quilt (figure 10).

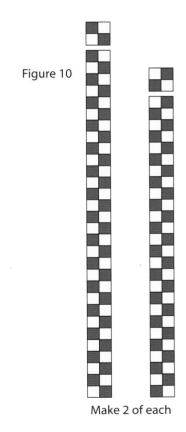

Figure 10

Make 2 of each

Add the taupe border 3 and red print border 4 to complete the quilt top (figure 11).

FINISHING

Layer and quilt as desired. Bind with double-fold, straight-grain binding and label your quilt.

Figure 11

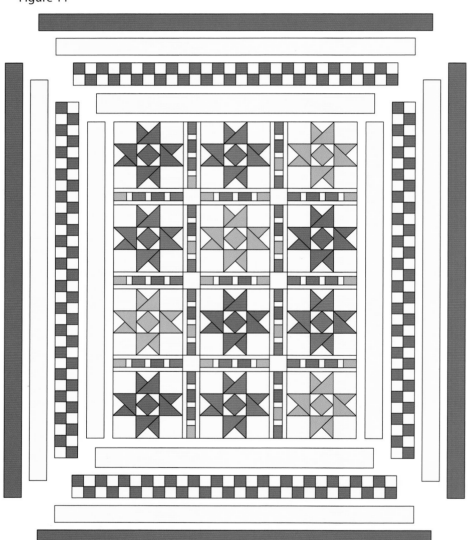

A secondary design is formed when a different fabric is used at the corners of the blocks.

Made and quilted by the author

Mary's Lucky Stars

Quilt size: 77½" x 88"
Finished block size: 9" x 9"

THOROLD PUBLIC LIBRARY

CUTTING INSTRUCTIONS
Use fabric at least 40" wide.

☆ Taupe   *Cut into:*

4 strips	3⅞" wide	40 A
5 strips	4¼" wide	45 B
16 strips	3½" wide	40 C, 12 strips for border 1 top & bottom & border 3
5 strips	2½" wide	18 E
4 strips	3¾" wide	(border 1 sides)

★ Green

4 strips	3⅞" wide	40 A
7 strips	1½" wide	160 D
2 strips	2½" wide	20 F
4 strips	4" wide	(strip-pieced border 2)
9 strips	3" wide	(border 4)

★ Pink

3 strips	3½" wide	30 C
7 strips	4¼"	61 B
4 strips	4" wide	(strip-pieced border 2)

☆ Gold

2 strips	4¼" wide	16 B
8 strips	2½" wide	31 E
★ Binding		10 strips 2½" wide
★ Backing		2 panels 42 " × 96"
★ Batting		81" × 96"

FABRIC REQUIREMENTS

Taupe	☆	3⅝ yards
Green	★	2¼ yards
Pink	★	1¾ yards
Gold	☆	1 yard
Binding	★	¾ yard
Backing	★	5¾ yards
Batting	★	81" × 96"

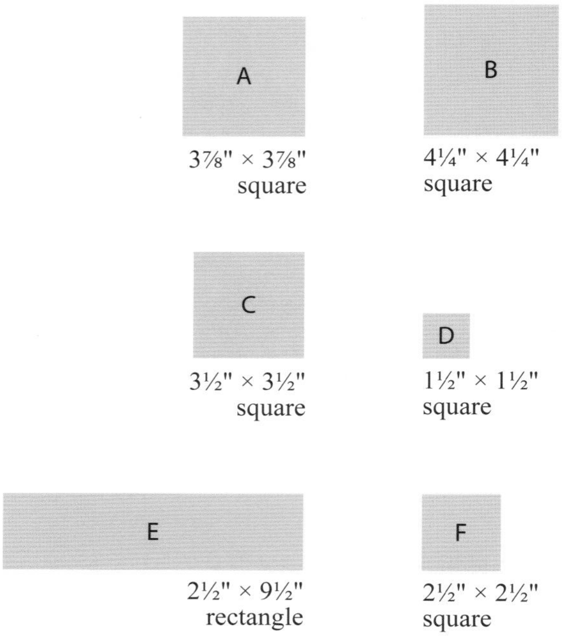

A

3⅞" × 3⅞"
square

B

4¼" × 4¼"
square

C

3½" × 3½"
square

D

1½" × 1½"
square

E

2½" × 9½"
rectangle

F

2½" × 2½"
square

CONSTRUCTION TECHNIQUES

Half-Square Triangles (page 87)
Quarter-Square Triangles (page 88)
Corner-Squares (page 90)
Border Application (page 91)

BLOCK CONSTRUCTION

Make 80 half-square triangles with 40 taupe A and 40 green A squares (figure 1).

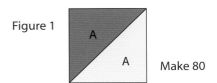

Figure 1 — Make 80

Make 58 two-color quarter-square triangles with 29 taupe B and 29 pink B squares (figure 2).

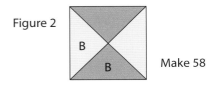

Figure 2 — Make 58

To make three-color quarter-square triangles, first make 32 half-square triangles with 16 pink B and 16 taupe B squares and make 32 half-square triangles with 16 pink B and 16 gold B squares. Pairing two different half-square triangles, make 62 quarter square triangles (figure 3). You will have two half-square triangle units left over.

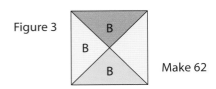

Figure 3 — Make 62

Referring to figure 4, assemble the blocks.

Figure 4

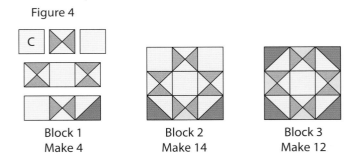

Block 1 — Make 4   Block 2 — Make 14   Block 3 — Make 12

SASHING CONSTRUCTION

Using the corner-square method, add two green D squares to one end of the taupe E rectangles (figure 5).

Figure 5 — Make 18

Using the corner-square method, add four green D squares to all four corners of the gold E rectangles (figure 6).

Figure 6 — Make 31

Referring to figure 7, make five sashing rows. Press the seam allowances away from the squares.

Figure 7

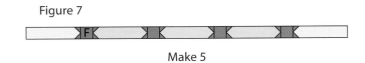

Make 5

QUILT TOP ASSEMBLY

Referring to figure 8, assemble the block rows. Pay careful attention to the orientation of blocks 1 and 2. Press the seam allowances toward the sashing strips.

Referring to figure 9, assemble the sashing and block rows. Press the seam allowances toward the sashing rows.

Figure 8

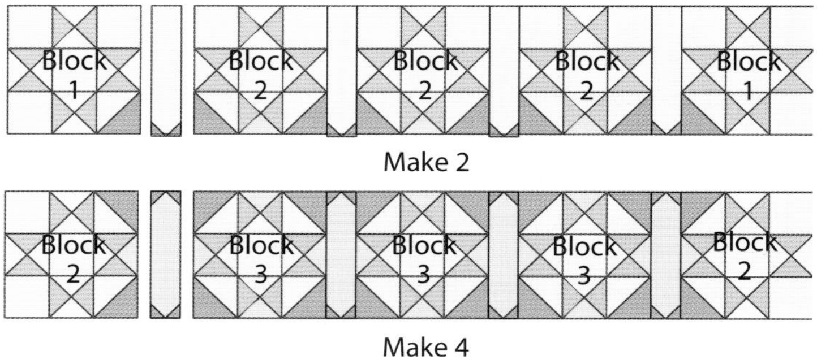

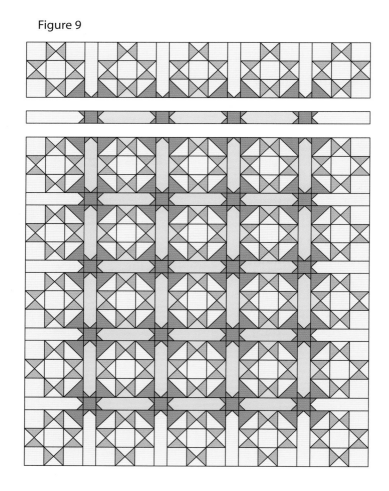

Figure 9

BORDER CONSTRUCTION

For the taupe border 1, add the 3¾" strips to the sides of the quilt, then add the 3½" strips to the top and bottom.

The top needs to measure 60" x 70½", including seam allowances, for the next border to fit.

Make four strip-sets, each with one green and one pink 4" strip (figure 10). Cut 39 segments 4".

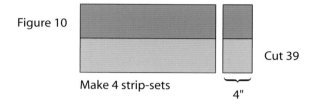

Figure 10

Make 4 strip-sets

Cut 39

4"

Join 10 of the segments for each border 2 side (figure 11).

Join nine segments for the top and bottom border 2. Separate the squares of the remaining segment and add the green square to the end of the top border and the pink square to the end of the bottom border (figure 12).

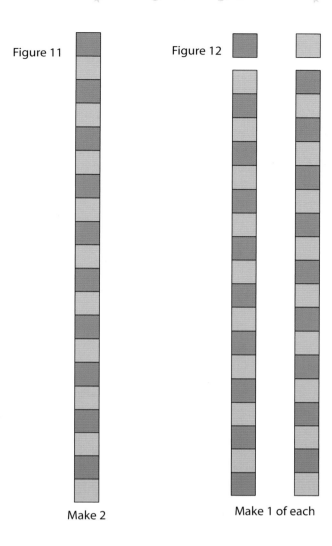

Figure 11

Figure 12

Make 2

Make 1 of each

Add the border 2 sides to the quilt. *Be sure that the green squares of both side strips are toward the bottom of the quilt when attaching them to the quilt.* Press the seam allowances toward the center of the quilt, then add the top and bottom border strips. If some of the borders don't quite fit, make minor adjustments in a few of the segment seams (figure 13).

Add the taupe border 3 and the green border 4 to complete the quilt top (figure 13).

Finishing

Layer and quilt as desired. Bind with double-fold, straight-grain binding and label your quilt.

Figure 13

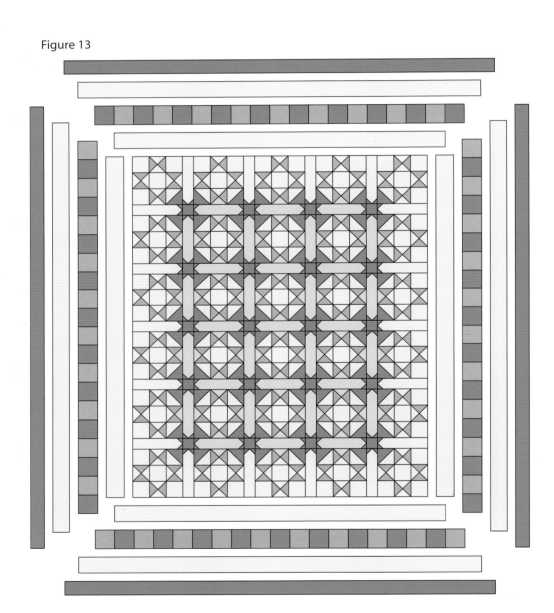

The corners of these Nine-Patch blocks are paper pieced to achieve perfect points. The pieced Snail's Trail border gives this quilt an interesting flair.

Made and quilted by the author

Heat Wave

Quilt size: 80" x 92"
Finished block size: 9" x 9"
Finished border block size: 6" x 6"

CUTTING INSTRUCTIONS
Use fabric at least 40" wide.

⭐ Brick

Cut into:

8 strips	2" wide	31 E
4 strips	2" wide	(strip piecing)
5 strips	2½" wide	(border 1)
9 strips	4½" wide	(border 6)

⭐ Gold

10 strips	2¾" wide	80 A
1 strip	2" wide	12 F

☆ Tan

15 strips	2¾" wide	192 B
4 strips	3" wide	48 D and 48 Dr (see cutting instructions in figure 5)
4 strips	2" wide	(strip piecing)
6 strips	3½" wide	(border 2)
4 strips	3¾" wide	(border 4 side borders)
4 strips	4½" wide	(border 4 top and bottom)

⭐ Green

4 strips	3¼" wide	48 C
1 strip	2" wide	(strip piecing)
7 strips	2" wide	(border 3)
⭐ Binding		10 strips 2½" wide
⭐ Backing		3 panels 30" × 100"
⭐ Batting		88" × 100"

FABRIC REQUIREMENTS

Brick	⭐	3¼ yards
Gold	⭐	2½ yards
Tan	☆	4½ yard
Green	⭐	1 yard
Binding	⭐	⅞ yard
Backing	⭐	8¾ yard
Batting	⭐	88" × 100"

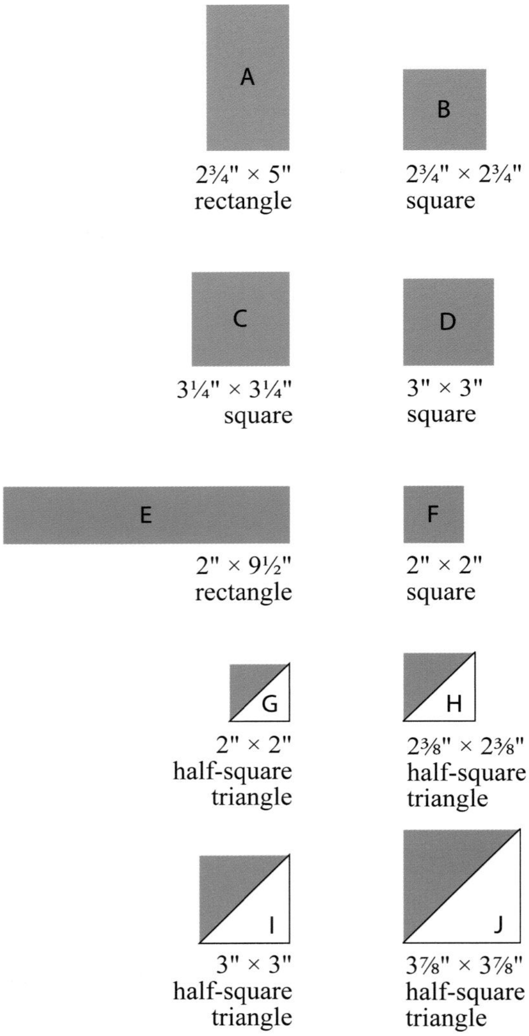

A
2¾" × 5"
rectangle

B
2¾" × 2¾"
square

C
3¼" × 3¼"
square

D
3" × 3"
square

E
2" × 9½"
rectangle

F
2" × 2"
square

G
2" × 2"
half-square triangle

H
2⅜" × 2⅜"
half-square triangle

I
3" × 3"
half-square triangle

J
3⅞" × 3⅞"
half-square triangle

CONSTRUCTION TECHNIQUES

Flying Geese (page 90)
Border Application (page 91)

BLOCK CONSTRUCTION

Make 80 flying-geese units with the gold A rectangles and tan B squares (figure 1).

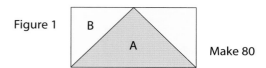

Figure 1   Make 80

Make two strip-sets, each with one tan and two brick 2" strips. Cut 40 segments 2" (figure 2).

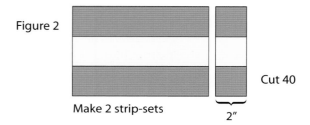

Figure 2   Make 2 strip-sets   2"   Cut 40

Make one strip-set with one green and two tan 2" strips. Cut 20 segments 2" (figure 3).

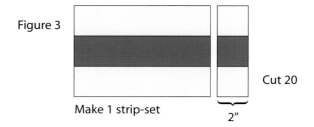

Figure 3   Make 1 strip-set   2"   Cut 20

Join the strip-set segments to make 20 nine-patch units (figure 4).

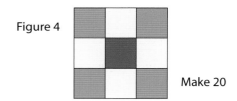

Figure 4   Make 20

With two squares wrong sides together, cut the 48 tan 3" squares as shown in figure 5 to make 48 D and 48 D-reverse pieces.

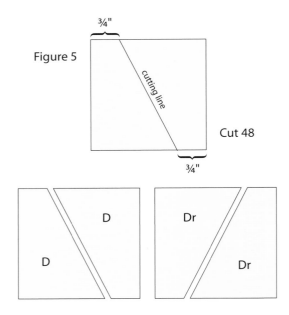

Figure 5

Cut 48

Make 48 copies of the paper-piecing template (figure 6).

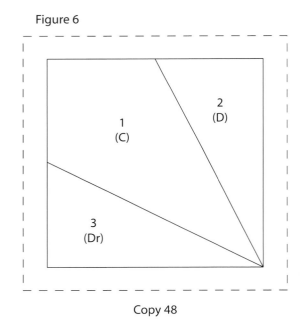

Figure 6

Copy 48

Paper-piece the corner units with the green C squares and the D and Dr pieces (figure 7). Trim to 2¾" x 2¾" and remove the paper.

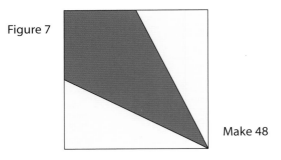

Figure 7

Make 48

Referring to figure 8, make 20 blocks.

Figure 8

Block 1
Make 4

Block 2
Make 10

Block 3
Make 6

Paying careful attention to the placement of the blocks, make five rows of blocks and E sashing strips (figure 9).

Figure 9

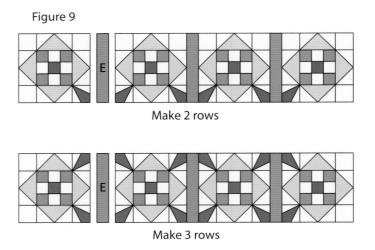

Make 2 rows

Make 3 rows

Make four sashing rows with the E sashing strips and F cornerstones (figure 10).

Figure 10

Make 4 rows

Referring to figure 11, join the sashing and block rows.

Figure 11

BORDER CONSTRUCTION

Add the brick border 1, tan border 2, and green border 3 (see figure 18, page 26).

For tan border 4, add the 3¾" strips to the sides of the quilt, then add the 4½" strips to the top and bottom (see figure 18, page 26).

For Snail's Trail border 5, cut the amounts shown out of both brick and tan. Cut the gold fabric as indicated.

⭐ Brick and Tan   *Cut into:*

2 strips	2" wide	24 ◻ 2" × 2" (total 48 G triangles)
2 strips	2⅜" wide	24 ◻ 2⅜" × 2⅜" (total 48 H triangles)
2 strips	3" wide	24 ◻ 3" × 3" (total 48 I triangles)
2 strips	3⅞" wide	24 ◻ 3⅞" × 3⅞" (total 48 J triangles)
2 strips	1¼" wide	(strip piecing)

⭐ Gold

3 strips	2" wide	48 ◻ 2" × 2" (total 96 G triangles)
3 strips	2⅜" wide	48 ◻ 2⅜" × 2⅜" (total 96 H triangles)
4 strips	3" wide	48 ◻ 3" × 3" (total 96 I triangles)
5 strips	3⅞" wide	8 ◻ 3⅞" × 3⅞" (total 96 J triangles)
2 strip sets	1¼" wide	(strip piecing)

The top needs to measure 60½" × 72½", including the seam allowances, for border 5 to fit.

Make two strip-sets, each with one brick and one gold 1¼" strip. Cut 48 segments 1¼" (figure 12).

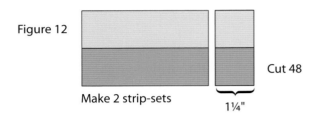

Figure 12

Cut 48

Make 2 strip-sets   1¼"

Make two strip-sets, each with one tan and one gold 1¼" strip. Cut 48 segments 1¼" (figure 13).

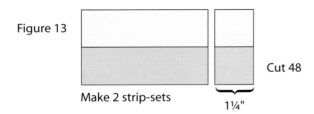

Figure 13

Cut 48

Make 2 strip-sets   1¼"

Join the segments to make 48 four-patch units (figure 14).

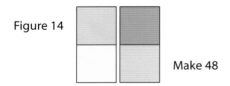

Figure 14

Make 48

Measure the four-patch units to make sure they are precisely 2" x 2". Adjust the seams if the units are too small or trim them to 2" square if they are too large.

Paying careful attention to the color placement, add the G triangles to the four-patch units (figure 15). Press after adding each triangle, pressing the seam allowances toward the outer point. After adding the fourth G triangle, the square should measure 2⅝" including seam allowances. Trim to that size if necessary.

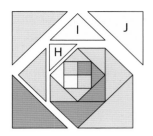

Figure 16

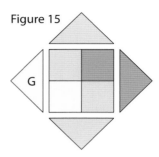

Figure 15

In the same manner, add the H triangles, then the I and J triangles (figure 16), checking the measurements given in the Checking Unit Size table after adding the fourth triangle of each size. Trim to size if necessary.

Checking Unit Size
(measurements include seam allowances)

After adding	Block should measure
G Triangles	2⅝" × 2⅝"
H Triangles	3½" × 3½"
I Triangles	4¾" × 4¾"
J Triangles	6½" × 6½"

Join 12 blocks for each of the four pieced borders, aligning them as shown in figure 17. Press the seam allowances open.

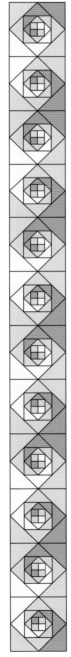

Figure 17

Make 4

Referring to figure 18, add the border 5 sides, then the top and bottom borders.

Add the brick border 6 to complete the quilt top.

FINISHING:

Layer and quilt as desired. Bind with the double-fold, straight-grain binding and label your quilt.

Figure 18

Made and quilted by the author

Quilt size: 71" x 91"
Finished block size: 10" x 10"

Puppet on a String

CUTTING INSTRUCTIONS
Use fabric at least 40" wide.

 Cream

		Cut into:
37 strips	2½" wide	350 A, 34 D, 9 strips for strip piecing
6 strips	2⅞" wide	72 C
7 strips	3½" wide	(border 1)

Gold

28 strips	2½"	69 A, 36 B, 68 D, 6 strips for strip piecing
4 strips	4½"	(strip piecing)

Green

9 strips 2½"	72 B

Red

6 strips	2⅞"	72 C
10 strips	2½"	(strip piecing)
9 strips	4"	(border 3)
★ Binding	9 strips 2½"
★ Backing	2 panels 40" × 99"
★ Batting	79" × 99"

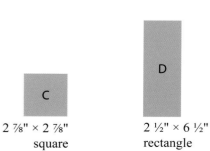

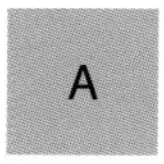

A
2 ½" × 2 ½"
square

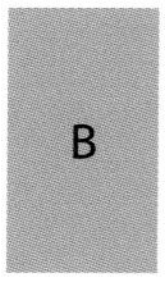

B
2 ½" × 4 ½"
rectangle

C
2 ⅞" × 2 ⅞"
square

D
2 ½" × 6 ½"
rectangle

FABRIC REQUIREMENTS

Cream	☆	4 yards
Gold	★	2¾ yards
Green	★	¾ yard
Red	★	2⅜ yard
Binding	★	¾ yard
Backing	★	5⅞ yard
Batting	★	79" × 99"

CONSTRUCTION TECHNIQUES

Flying Geese (page 89)
Half-Square Triangles (page 87)
Border Application (page 91)

BLOCK CONSTRUCTION

Block 1

Make 72 flying-geese units with the green B rectangles and 144 cream A squares (figure 1).

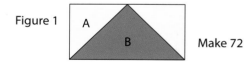

Figure 1   Make 72

Make 144 half-square triangle units with the cream C and red C squares (figure 2).

Figure 2   Make 144

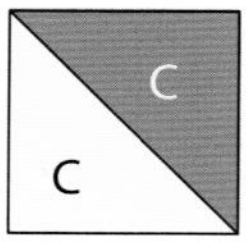

Join two half-square triangles, then add a flying-geese unit to make 72 block 1 corner units (figure 3).

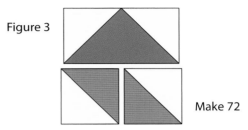

Figure 3

Make 72

Make two strip-sets, each with one cream 2½" strip and two gold 4½" strips. Cut 18 segments 2½"(figure 4).

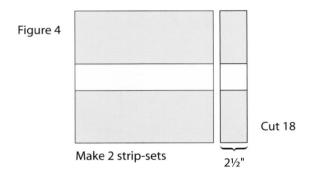

Figure 4

Cut 18

Make 2 strip-sets

2½"

Referring to figure 5, assemble 18 block 1.

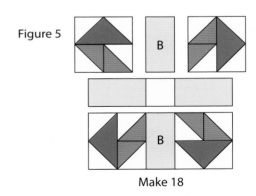

Figure 5

B

B

Make 18

Block 2

Using the corner square method, make 34 modified flying-geese units with the cream D rectangles and 68 gold A squares (figure 6). Note that the triangles do not meet in the center of the unit.

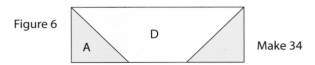

Figure 6

D

A

Make 34

Using the corner square method, make 68 modified flying-geese units with the gold D rectangles and 136 cream A squares (figure 7).

Figure 7

D

A

Make 68

Make a strip-set with one gold and two cream 2½" strips. You need 17 segments 2½". Cut 16 from the strip-set and make the last segment with one gold A and two cream A squares (figure 8).

Figure 8

Cut 16

Make 2 strip-sets

2½"

Referring to figure 9, assemble 17 block 2.

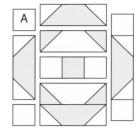

Figure 9

Make 17

Arrange the blocks in an alternating pattern and join the rows (figure 10).

The quilt needs to measure 50½" x 70½ for the pieced border to fit. If needed, trim to size.

Figure 10

BORDER CONSTRUCTION

Add the cream border 1 to the quilt (see figure 14 on page 32).

Referring to figure 11, make five strip-sets, each with a red 2½" strip and a cream 2½" strip. Cut 68 segments 2½".

Make five strip-sets each with a gold 2½" strip and a red 2½" strip. Cut 72 segments 2½".

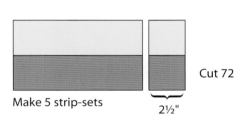

Figure 11

Make 5 strip-sets   2½"   Cut 68

Make 5 strip-sets   2½"   Cut 72

Join the strip-set segments to make 70 four-patch units (figure 12).

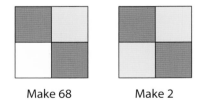

Figure 12

Make 68   Make 2

Join 19 four-patch units for the side borders. Join 16 four-patch units for the top and bottom borders, placing a gold and red four-patch unit at one end of each strip as shown (figure 13).

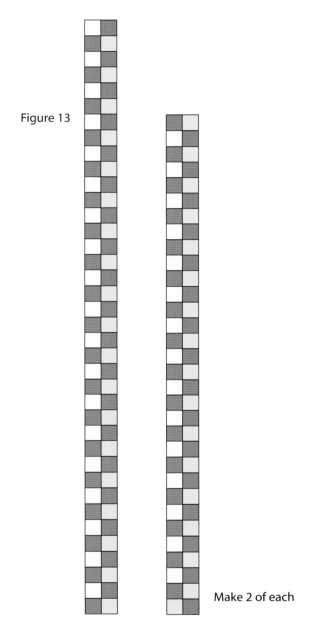

Figure 13

Make 2 of each

Add the four-patch borders to the quilt, placing them as shown in figure 14. Press the seam allowances toward the center of the quilt.

Add the red border 3 to complete the quilt top (figure 14).

Finishing

Layer and quilt as desired. Bind with the double-fold, straight-grain binding and label your quilt.

Figure 14

This is a great quilt for fat quarters, plus yardage for the background and the alternate Nine-Patch blocks.

Made by Vicky McGee of Upland, California. Quilted by the author.

Pinwheel Garden

Quilt size: 74" x 92"
Finished block size: 9" x 9"
Finished border block size: 5" x 9"

CUTTING INSTRUCTIONS
Use fabric at least 40" wide.

⭐ 12 assorted Fat Quarters

Cut 5 fat quarters into the amounts shown. Cut 7 fat quarters into half the amounts shown.

8 B, 8 C, 4 D, 4 H

☆ Cream		*Cut into:*
15 strips	3½" wide	72 A, 8 strips for border 5
12 strips	2" wide	68 B, 8 strips for border 1
5 strips	2⅜" wide	68 C
4 strips	4¼" wide	34 D
5 strips	2⅛" wide	72 E
4 strips	5½" wide	56 G for pieced border 4, 4 I
5 strips	5⅞" wide	28 H for pieced border 4
7 strips	1½" wide	(border 3)

⭐ Brown

7 strips	3½" wide	17 A, 72 F
8 strips	2" wide	144 B

⭐ Red

2 strips	3½" wide	18 A
16 strips	2½" wide	(borders 2 and 6)
⭐ Binding		9 strips 2½"
⭐ Backing		2 panels 40" × 100"
⭐ Batting		80" × 100"

FABRIC REQUIREMENTS

12 Assorted Fat Quarters	⭐	
Cream	☆	5¼ yards
Brown	⭐	1¼ yards
Red	⭐	1½ yard
Binding	⭐	¾ yard
Backing	⭐	5⅞ yards
Batting	⭐	80" × 100"

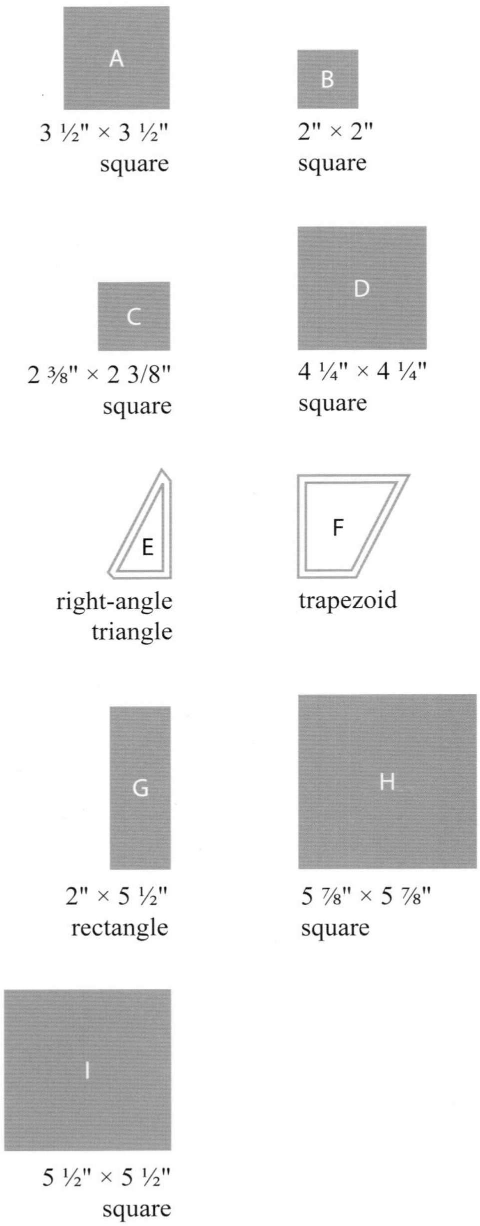

A
3 ½" × 3 ½"
square

B
2" × 2"
square

C
2 ⅜" × 2 3/8"
square

D
4 ¼" × 4 ¼"
square

E
right-angle
triangle

F
trapezoid

G
2" × 5 ½"
rectangle

H
5 ⅞" × 5 ⅞"
square

I
5 ½" × 5 ½"
square

CONSTRUCTION TECHNIQUES

Half-Square Triangles (page 87)
Quarter-Square Triangles (page 88)
Corner-Squares (page 90)
Border Application (page 91)

ADDITIONAL MATERIALS

Template plastic

BLOCK CONSTRUCTION

Block 1

These instructions are for one block since this is a scrappy quilt.

Make two of block 1 with each of five fat quarters and one block 1 with each of the remaining seven fat quarters.

Make eight half-square triangle units with the assorted fat quarters and cream C squares (figure 1).

Figure 1   Make 8

Make four quarter-square triangle units with the assorted fat quarters and cream D squares (figure 2).

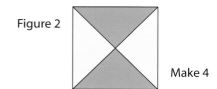

Figure 2

Make 4

Referring to figure 3, assemble block 1.

Repeat these steps for a total of 17 block 1.

Block 2

Trace the E and F templates on template plastic and cut them out on the drawn line.

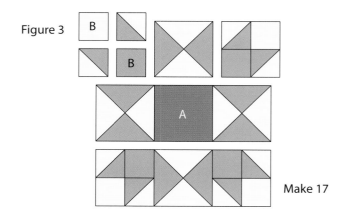

Figure 3

B

B

A

Make 17

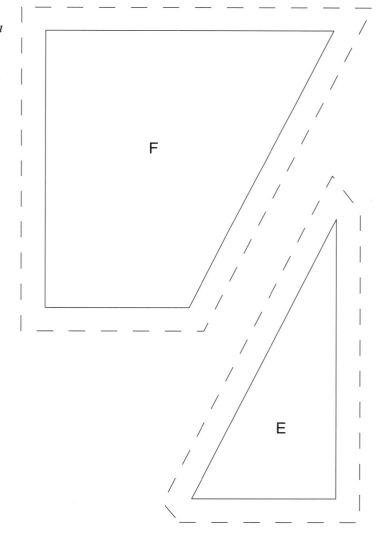

F

E

With the template and fabric both right side up, cut 72 E triangles from the 2⅛" cream strips (figure 4).

With the template and fabric both right side up, cut 72 F pieces from the brown 3½" strips (figure 5).

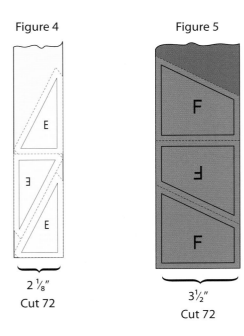

Figure 4

Figure 5

E

E

E

F

F

F

2⅛"

Cut 72

3½"

Cut 72

Be sure to cut with both the templates and fabric right side up or the pieces will be backward.

Join the E and F pieces to make the block 2 corner units (figure 6).

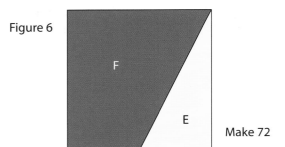

Figure 6

F

E

Make 72

If you would prefer to paper-piece these corner units, a template is provided below

Use the corner-square method to make the units shown in figure 7.

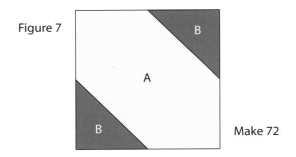

Figure 7

B

A

B

Make 72

Referring to figure 8, assemble block 2.

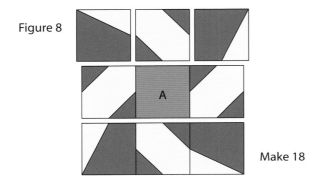

Figure 8

A

Make 18

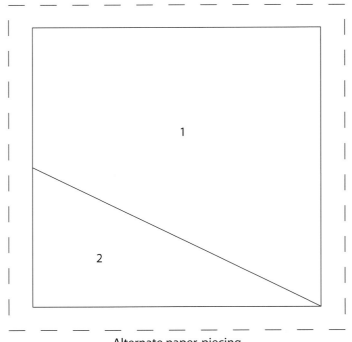

1

2

Alternate paper-piecing template

QUILT TOP ASSEMBLY

Arrange the blocks in an alternating pattern as shown in figure 9. Join the blocks into rows and then join the rows.

Add the cream border 1, red border 2, and cream border 3 (see figure 14 on page 38).

The quilt needs to measure 54½" x 72½ for the pieced border to fit. If needed, trim to size.

For the pieced border 4, make 56 half-square triangles with 28 assorted fat quarters and 28 cream H squares (figure 10). (You'll have some fat quarters H squares left over.)

Figure 10

Make 56 assorted half-square triangles

Lay two matching half-square triangles side-by-side as shown in figure 11. Starting at the center peaks, cut three 1½" strips from each half-square triangle. (The outer 1" strip will not be used.)

Figure 11

Center peaks

1"   1½"   1½"   1"

Cut 28 pairs of assorted half square triangles

Figure 9

Arrange the strips as shown in figure 12 and join them with two cream G rectangles. Press the center seam open and the other seams towards the nearest outside edges.

Measure and check that the border blocks are 5½" x 9½".

Figure 12

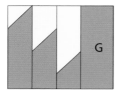

Join strips with G rectangles

Join eight blocks for the border sides and six blocks plus two cream I squares for the top and bottom borders (figure 13).

Figure 13

Make 2 of each

Add border 4 to the quilt (figure 14).

Add the cream border 5 and red border 6 to complete the quilt top (figure 14).

FINISHING

Layer and quilt as desired. Bind with double-fold, straight-grain binding and label your quilt.

Figure 14

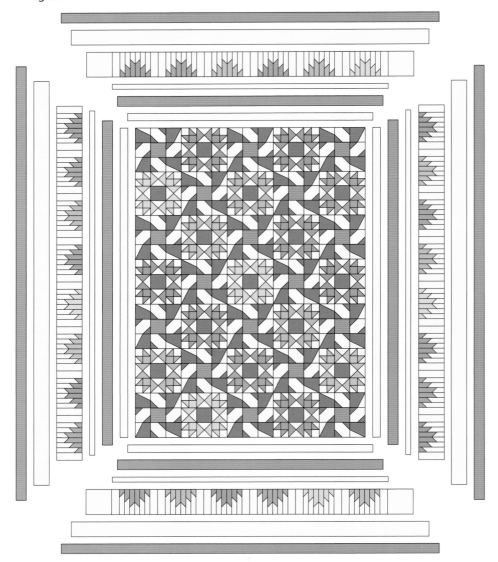

Made and quilted by the author

KEEP IN
Touch
Quilt size: 76" x 92"
Finished block size: 9" x 9"

CUTTING INSTRUCTIONS
Use fabric at least 40" wide.

☆ Tan

		Cut into:
13 strips	3½" wide	72 A, 4 E, 10 F
2 strips	3⅞" wide	12 D
3 strips	5¼" wide	16 G
3 strips	2" wide	(border 2 top & bottom)
4 strips	3" wide	(border 2 sides)
8 strips	4" wide	(border 4)

★ Green

4 strips	3½" wide	72 C
8 strips	3⅞" wide	72 D
1 strip	4½" wide	4 I
3 strips	5¼" wide	16 G

★ Rose

11 strips	2" wide	216 B
2 strips	3½" wide	17 A
7 strips	3⅞" wide	70 D
4 strips	4⅞" wide	32 H
9 strips	3" wide	(border 5)

☆ Stripe

6 strips	3½" wide	18 A, 72 C
★ Binding		10 strips 2½"
★ Backing		2 panels 40" × 100"
★ Batting		80" × 100"

FABRIC REQUIREMENTS

Tan	☆	3⅝ yards
Green	★	2 yards
Rose	★	3 yards
Stripe	☆	¾ yard
Binding	★	¾ yard
Backing	★	5⅞ yards
Batting	★	80" × 100"

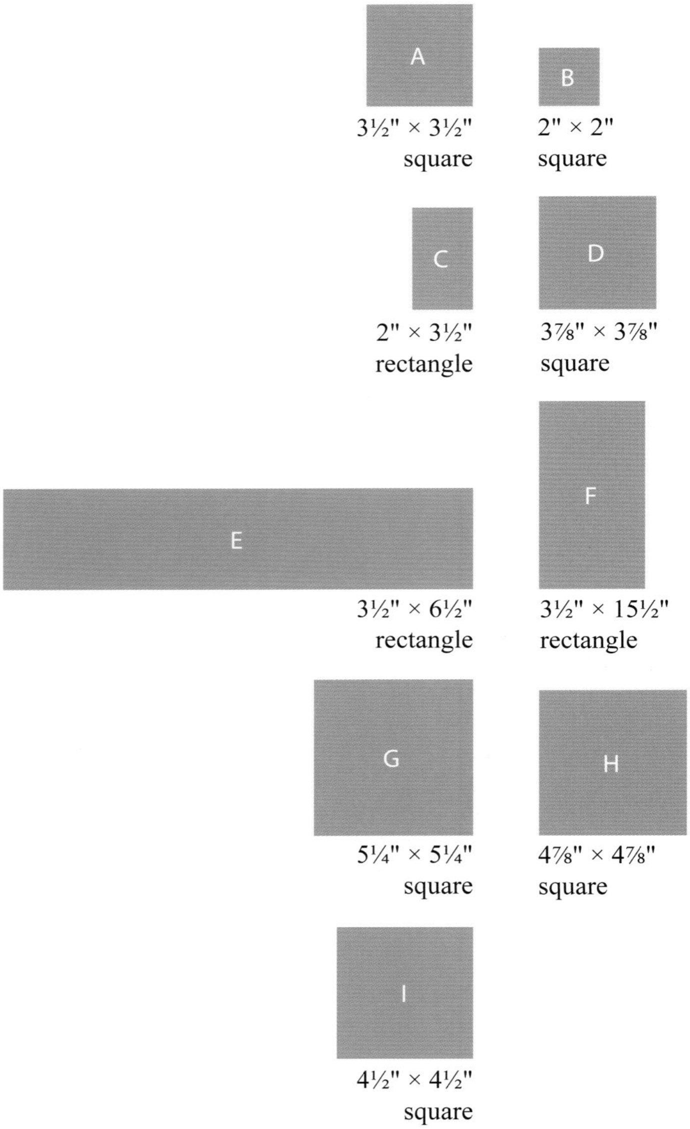

A
3½" × 3½" square

B
2" × 2" square

C
2" × 3½" rectangle

D
3⅞" × 3⅞" square

E
3½" × 6½" rectangle

F
3½" × 15½" rectangle

G
5¼" × 5¼" square

H
4⅞" × 4⅞" square

I
4½" × 4½" square

CONSTRUCTION TECHNIQUES

Corner-Squares (Square-in-a-Square) (page 90)
Flying Geese (page 89)
Half-Square Triangles (page 87)
Partial Quarter-Square Triangles (page 89)
Border Application (page 91)

BLOCK CONSTRUCTION

Use the corner-square method to make 18 square-in-a-square units with the stripe A and rose B squares (figure 1).

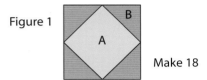

Figure 1

Make 18

Make 72 flying geese units with the stripe C rectangles and rose B squares (figure 2).

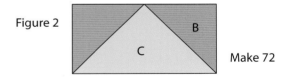

Figure 2

Make 72

Make 130 half-square triangles with the green D and rose D squares (figure 3).

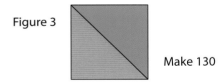

Figure 3

Make 130

Make 10 half-square triangles with the tan D and rose D squares (figure 4).

Figure 4

Make 10

Referring to figure 5, make the blocks.

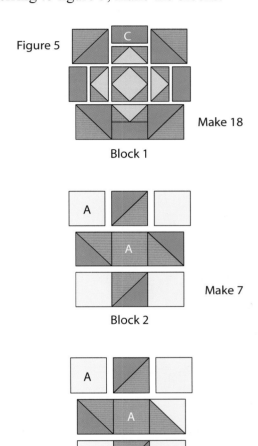

Figure 5

Make 18

Block 1

Make 7

Block 2

Make 10

Block 3

QUILT TOP CONSTRUCTION

Arrange the blocks as shown in figure 6, paying careful attention to the orientation of block 3. Press the seam allowances away from block 1.

Figure 6

Make 14 half-square triangles with the green D and tan D squares (figure 7).

Figure 7

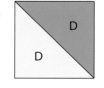

Make 14

Assemble border 1 as shown in figure 8.

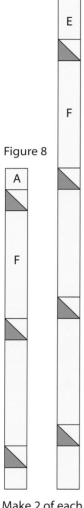

Figure 8

Make 2 of each

Add border 1 to the quilt (see figure 11, page 44). Note that the top and bottom borders are added first. Press the seam allowances toward the outside edges of the quilt.

For the tan border 2, add the 3" strips to the sides of the quilt, then add the 2" strips to the top and bottom (see figure 11, page 44). Press the seam allowances toward the outside edges of the quilt.

The quilt needs to measure 56½" x 72½" for the pieced border to fit. If needed, trim to size.

Make 64 partial quarter-square triangles with the green G and tan G squares and the rose H squares (figure 9).

Figure 9

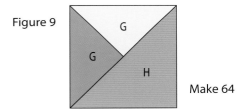

Make 64

Join 18 partial quarter-square triangles for the border 3 sides, alternating their position as shown in figure 10. Join 14 partial quarter-square triangles plus the green I squares for the top and bottom borders.

Figure 10

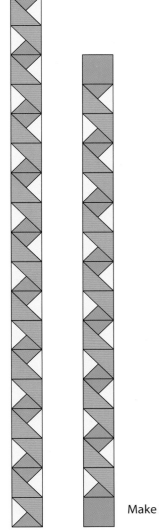

Make 2 of each

Referring to figure 11, add border 3 to the quilt. Add the tan border 4 and rose border 5 to complete the quilt top.

FINISHING

Layer and quilt as desired. Bind with double-fold, straight-grain binding and label your quilt.

Figure 11

The ribbon effect is created by using three values of the same color. The wide outer border is an excellent area to showcase interesting quilting.

Made and quilted by the author

Stars and Streamers

Quilt size: 70" x 88"
Finished block size: 9" x 9"

CUTTING INSTRUCTIONS
Use fabric at least 40" wide.

Magenta   *Cut into:*

16 strips	3½" wide	170 A
13 strips	3⅞" wide	123 B
6 strips	2" wide	(border 1)
8 strips	5½" wide	(border 3)

Light Green

2 strips	3½" wide	17 A
1 strip	3⅞" wide	9 B

Medium Green

2 strips	3½" wide	17 A
2 strips	3⅞" wide	16 B

Dark Green

2 strips	3½" wide	17 A
2 strips	3⅞" wide	8 B

Gold

6 strips	3⅞" wide	54 B

Lavender

2 strips 3½" wide		18 A
4 strips 3⅞" wide		36 B
Binding		9 strips 2½"
Backing		2 panels 39" × 96"
Batting		78" × 96"

FABRIC REQUIREMENTS

Magenta	★	4⅞ yards
Light Green	★	½ yard
Medium Green	★	⅝ yard
Dark Green	★	½ yard
Gold	★	⅞ yard
Lavender	★	¾ yard
Binding	★	¾ yard
Backing	★	5⅝ yards
Batting	★	78" × 96"

3½" × 3½"
square

3⅞" × 3⅞"
square

CONSTRUCTION TECHNIQUES

Half-Square Triangles (page 87)
Border Application (page 91)

BLOCK CONSTRUCTION

Referring to figure 1, make half-square triangles with the B squares.

Figure 1

| Make 24 | Make 17 | Make 32 | Make 15 | Make 72 |

Join the half-square triangles and A squares to make the blocks (figure 2).

Pressing Instructions

By pressing as indicated, the seams in your rows and blocks will "nest," making it easier to match the points.

Press toward the center square in the middle row of all blocks. Press away from the center in the top and bottom block rows.

Press the row seams of block 1 away from the center.

Press the row seams of blocks 2–6 toward the center.

When joining the blocks, press all seams toward block 1.

Figure 2

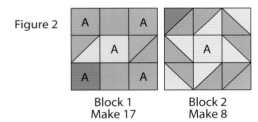

Block 1
Make 17

Block 2
Make 8

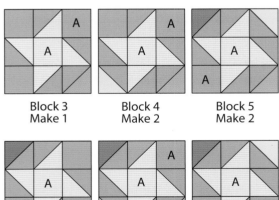

Block 3
Make 1

Block 4
Make 2

Block 5
Make 2

Block 6
Make 1

Block 7
Make 2

Block 8
Make 2

Arrange the blocks as shown in figure 3. Check the orientation of each block against figure 7 (page 49) to be sure it is positioned correctly.

Figure 3

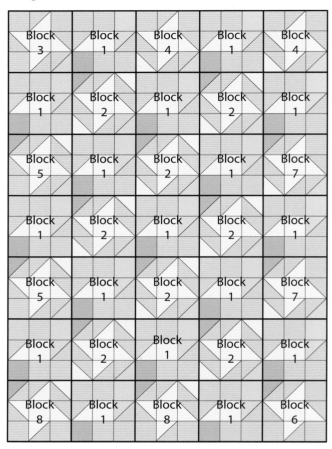

BORDER CONSTRUCTION

Add the magenta border 1 to the quilt.

The quilt needs to measure 48½" x 66½" for the pieced border to fit. If needed, trim to size.

For pieced border 2, make 84 half-square triangles with the remaining magenta B and gold B squares (figure 4).

Figure 4   B   B   Make 84

Join the half-square triangles and magenta A squares to make 42 four-patch units (figure 5).

Figure 5

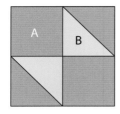

A   B   Make 42

Join 11 four-patch units for each border side and 10 four-patch units for the top and bottom borders. Note that the orientation of the four-patch units in the side borders is different from the top and bottom borders (figure 6). Add to the quilt.

Figure 6

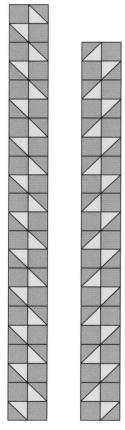

Make 2 of each

Add border 2 to the quilt. Add the magenta border 3 to complete the quilt top (figure 7).

Finishing

Layer and quilt as desired. Bind with the double-fold, straight-grain binding and label your quilt.

Figure 7

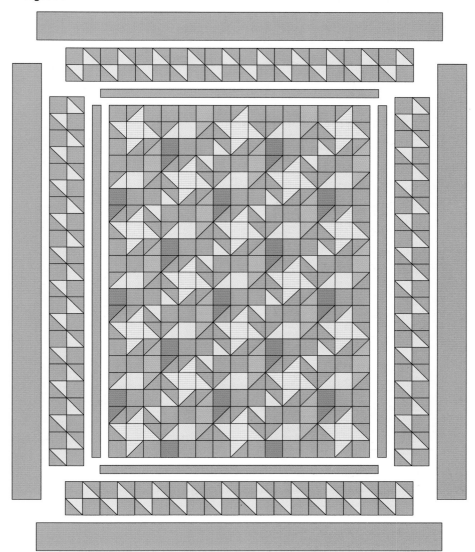

 Hourglass Surrounded

Quilt size: 62" x 78"
Finished block size: 8" x 8"

The pieced border surrounding the blocks appears to float over the background. This is a two-block quilt, although there are five versions of one of the blocks.

Made and quilted by the author

CUTTING INSTRUCTIONS
Use fabric at least 40" wide.

Cream | Cut into:

2 strips	5¼" wide	9 A
3 strips	4½" wide	17 E

Goldish Red

2 strips	5¼" wide	14 A
18 strips	2½" wide	68 B, 136 C
3 strips	2⅞" wide	34 D

Dark Red

14 strips	2½" wide	68 B, 68 C
3 strips	2⅞" wide	34 D
4 strips	4⅞" wide	30 H

Green

2 strips	2½" wide	14 B
3 strips	2⅞" wide	36 D

Black

4 strips	5¼" wide	23 A
3 strips	2⅞" wide	36 D
24 strips	2½" wide	164 C, 4 F, 10 G (7 strips for border 2)
1 strip	4⅞" wide	2 H
8 strips	3½" wide	(border 4)
★ Binding		8 strips 2½"
★ Backing		2 panels 35" × 86"
★ Batting		70" × 86"

FABRIC REQUIREMENTS

Cream	★	⅞ yard
Goldish Red	★	1⅞ yards
Dark Red	★	1⅞ yards
Green	★	½ yard
Black	★	3⅝ yards
Binding	★	⅝ yard
Backing	★	5 yards
Batting	★	70" × 86"

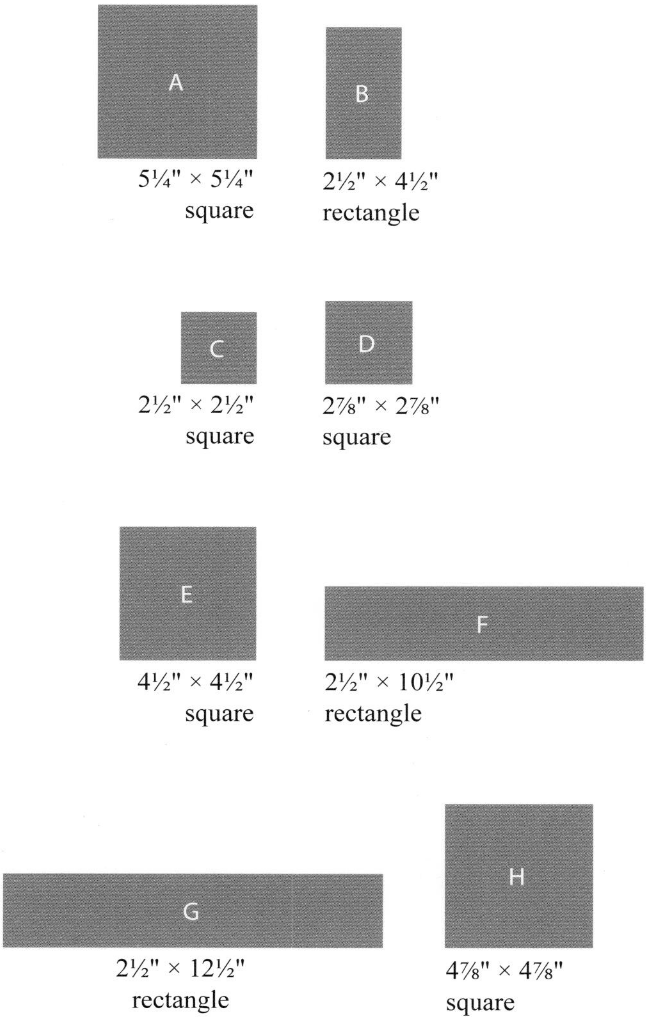

A
5¼" × 5¼"
square

B
2½" × 4½"
rectangle

C
2½" × 2½"
square

D
2⅞" × 2⅞"
square

E
4½" × 4½"
square

F
2½" × 10½"
rectangle

G
2½" × 12½"
rectangle

H
4⅞" × 4⅞"
square

CONSTRUCTION TECHNIQUES

Quarter-Square Triangles (page 88)
Flying Geese (page 89)
Square-in-a-Square (page 90)
Half-Square Triangles (page 87)
Partial Quarter-Square Triangles (page 89)
Border Application (page 91)

BLOCK CONSTRUCTION

Blocks 1 through 5

Make 18 quarter-square triangles with the cream A and black A squares (figure 1).

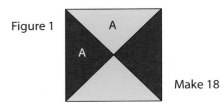

Figure 1

Make 18

Make 68 flying-geese units with the goldish red B rectangles and black C squares (figure 2). Ten of these units will be used in border 1.

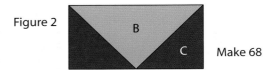

Figure 2

Make 68

Make 14 flying-geese units with the green B rectangles and black C squares (figure 3).

Figure 3

Make 14

Make 72 half-square triangles with the green D and black D squares (figure 4).

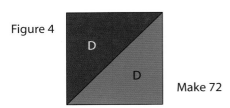

Figure 4

Make 72

Referring to figure 5, assemble blocks 1–5.

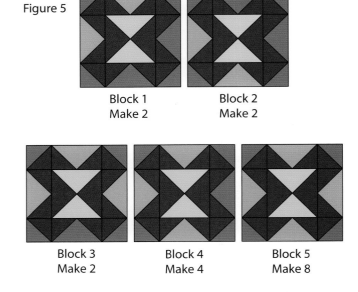

Figure 5

Block 1
Make 2

Block 2
Make 2

Block 3
Make 2

Block 4
Make 4

Block 5
Make 8

Block 6

Using the corner-square method, make 17 square-in-a-square units with the cream E squares and dark red C squares (figure 6).

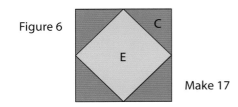

Figure 6

Make 17

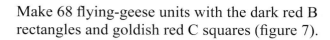

Make 68 flying-geese units with the dark red B rectangles and goldish red C squares (figure 7).

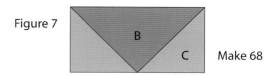

Figure 7 — Make 68

Make 68 half-square triangles with goldish red and dark red D squares (figure 8).

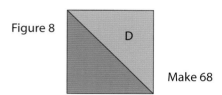

Figure 8 — Make 68

Referring to figure 9, assemble block 6.

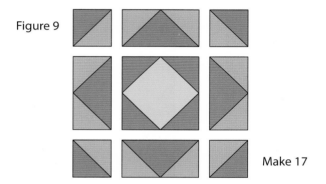

Figure 9 — Make 17

QUILT TOP AND BORDER CONSTRUCTION

Lay out the blocks as shown in figure 10. Check the orientation of the blocks along the outer edges to be sure they are positioned correctly (see figure 15 on page 55). Join the blocks into rows and join the rows.

Figure 10

Make the border 1 strips as shown in figure 11 and add to the quilt.

Figure 11

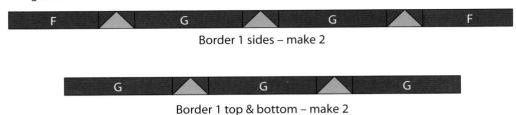

Border 1 sides – make 2

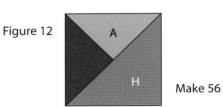

Border 1 top & bottom – make 2

Add the black border 2 to the quilt.

The quilt needs to measure 48½" x 64½" for the pieced border to fit. If needed, trim to size.

Make 56 partial quarter-square triangles with 14 goldish red A and 14 black A squares and 28 dark red H squares (figure 12).

Figure 12

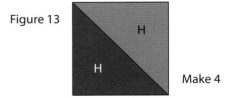

Make 56

Make four half-square triangles with two dark red H and two black H squares (figure 13).

Figure 13

Make 4

Join 16 partial quarter-square triangles to form each border 3 side. Join 12 partial quarter-square triangles plus two of the half-square triangles to make the border 3 top and bottom (figure 14).

Figure 14

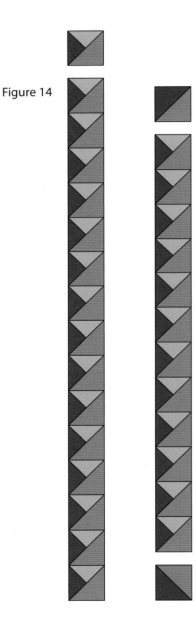

Make 2 of each

Add border 3 as shown in the quilt top assembly diagram. Add the black border 4 to complete the quilt top (figure 15).

FINISHING

Layer and quilt as desired. Bind with the double-fold, straight-grain binding and label your quilt.

Figure 15

Field of Jewels

Made and quilted by the author

Quilt size: 66" x 78"
Finished block size: 10" x 10"

CUTTING INSTRUCTIONS
Use fabric at least 40" wide.

★ **7 Assorted Fat Quarters**

From each of 6 fat quarters, cut: 12 B, 6 D

From the 7th fat quarter, cut: 8 B, 4 D

Gold		Cut into:
4 strips	2½" wide	51 A
16 strips	1½" wide	408 C
7 strips	1½" wide	(border 3)

☆ **White**

2 strips	1½" wide	36 C
5 strips	4⅞" wide	40 D
7 strips	2½" wide	14 E, 4 H
1 strip	3¼" wide	4 F
7 strips	3½" wide	(border 2)

★ **Black**

9 strips	2½" wide	38 B, 12 E
1 strip	3¼" wide	4 F
1 strip	2⅞" wide	7 G
8 strips	4½" wide	(border 4)
★ Binding		8 strips 2½"
★ Backing		2 panels 37" × 86"
★ Batting		74" × 86"

FABRIC REQUIREMENTS

7 Assorted Fat Quarters ★
Gold	☆	1½ yards
White	☆	2¼ yards
Black	★	2 yards
Binding	★	¾ yard
Backing	★	5 yards
Batting	★	74" × 86"

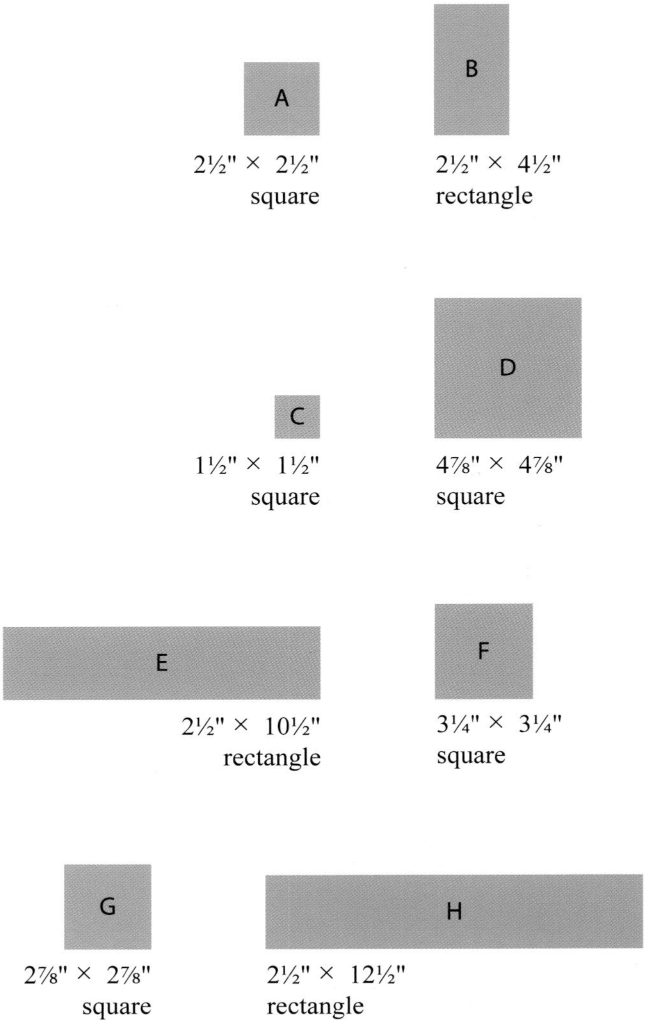

A
2½" × 2½"
square

B
2½" × 4½"
rectangle

C
1½" × 1½"
square

D
4⅞" × 4⅞"
square

E
2½" × 10½"
rectangle

F
3¼" × 3¼"
square

G
2⅞" × 2⅞"
square

H
2½" × 12½"
rectangle

CONSTRUCTION TECHNIQUES

Corner-Squares (page 90)
Half-Square Triangles (page 87)
Partial Quarter-Square Triangles(page 89)
Border Application (page 91)

BLOCK CONSTRUCTION

Make the corner-square units as shown in figure 1 with the assorted B rectangles and 248 gold C squares.

Figure 1

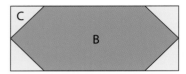

Make 62 assorted

Make the corner-square units as shown in figure 2 with the assorted B rectangles and 36 each gold C and white C squares.

Figure 2

Make 18 assorted

Two of these corner-square units will be used in each of the corner blocks. One of these corner-square units will be used in each of the blocks along the sides of your quilt.

Make 80 half-square triangles with the white D and assorted D squares (figure 3).

Figure 3

Make 80 assorted

Plan carefully if you do not want to have two blocks of the same color together. Using a design wall is helpful in planning your layout.

Make 20 blocks using corner-square units, the half-square triangles, and 20 A squares (figure 4).

Figure 4

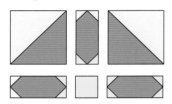

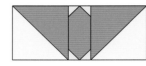

Block 1
Make 4

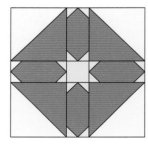

Block 2
Make 10

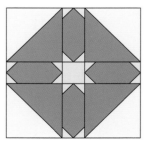

Block 3
Make 6

QUILT TOP ASSEMBLY

Make 38 corner-square units with black B rectangles and gold C squares (figure 5).

Figure 5   Make 38

Make 12 corner-square units with black E rectangles and the remaining gold C squares (figure 6).

Figure 6   Make 12

Make 15 block-sashing units and 4 row-sashing units with the corner-square units and the gold A squares (figure 7).

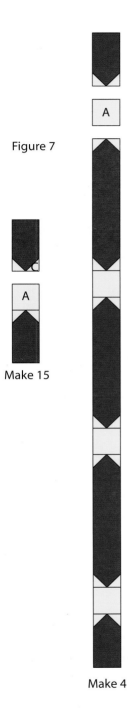

Figure 7

Make 15

Make 4

Arrange and join the blocks and sashing units as shown in figure 8, positioning block 1 at the corners, block 2 along the sides, and block 3 in the center. Pay careful attention to the orientations of the blocks.

Figure 8

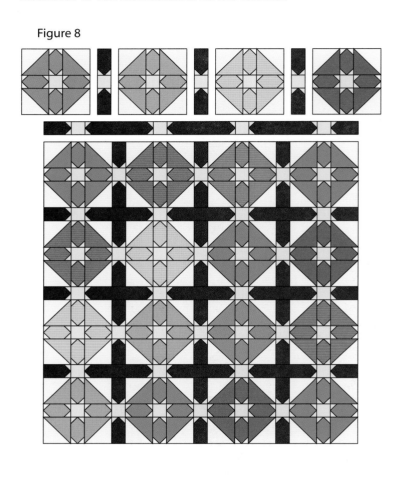

Join the partial quarter-square triangles with the white E and white H rectangles to make the border 1 units as shown in figure 10.

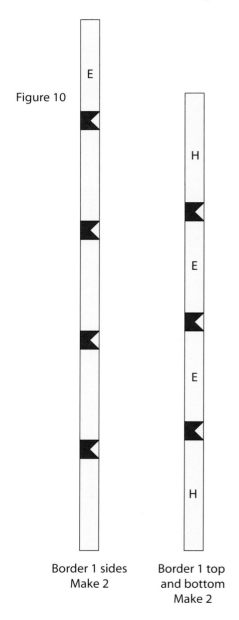

Figure 10

Border 1 sides
Make 2

Border 1 top
and bottom
Make 2

BORDERS

Make 14 partial quarter-square triangles with the black F and white F squares and the black G squares (figure 9).

Figure 9

Make 14

Add the side borders first. Press the seam allowances toward the border. Add the top and bottom borders. Press as before.

Add the white border 2, gold border 3, and black border 4 to complete the quilt top (figure 11).

FINISHING

Layer and quilt as desired. Bind using double-fold, straight-grain binding and label your quilt.

Figure 11

★ Star Struck

Secondary stars are created by the sashing.

Made and quilted by the author

Quilt size: 66" x 78"
Finished block size: 9" x 9"

CUTTING INSTRUCTIONS
Use fabric at least 40" wide.

☆ Tan | Cut into:

8 strips	3½" wide	80 A
5 strips	4¼" wide	40 B
8 strips	2½" wide	31 C
1 strip	2¾" wide	18 G

★ Print

2 strips	3½" wide	20 A
5 strips	4¼" wide	40 B

☆ Gold

4 strips	1½" wide	96 D
17 strips	2½" wide	132 E, 58 K

★ Light Green

2 strips	1½" wide	28 D
14 strips	2½" wide	4 H, 4 I, 14 J, 58 K
3 strips	2¼" wide	18 F, 18 Fr
3 strips	3½" wide	(border 2)
3 strips	4" wide	(border 2)

★ Dark Green

8 strips	2½" wide	116 E
1 strip	4½" wide	4 L
8 strips	3½" wide	(border 4)
★ Binding		8 strips 2½"
★ Backing		2 panels 37" × 86"
★ Batting		74" × 86"

FABRIC REQUIREMENTS

Tan	☆	2¼ yards
Print	★	1 yard
Gold	★	1½ yards
Light Green	★	2⅛ yards
Dark Green	★	1¾ yards
Binding	★	⅝ yard
Backing	★	5 yards
Batting	★	74" × 86"

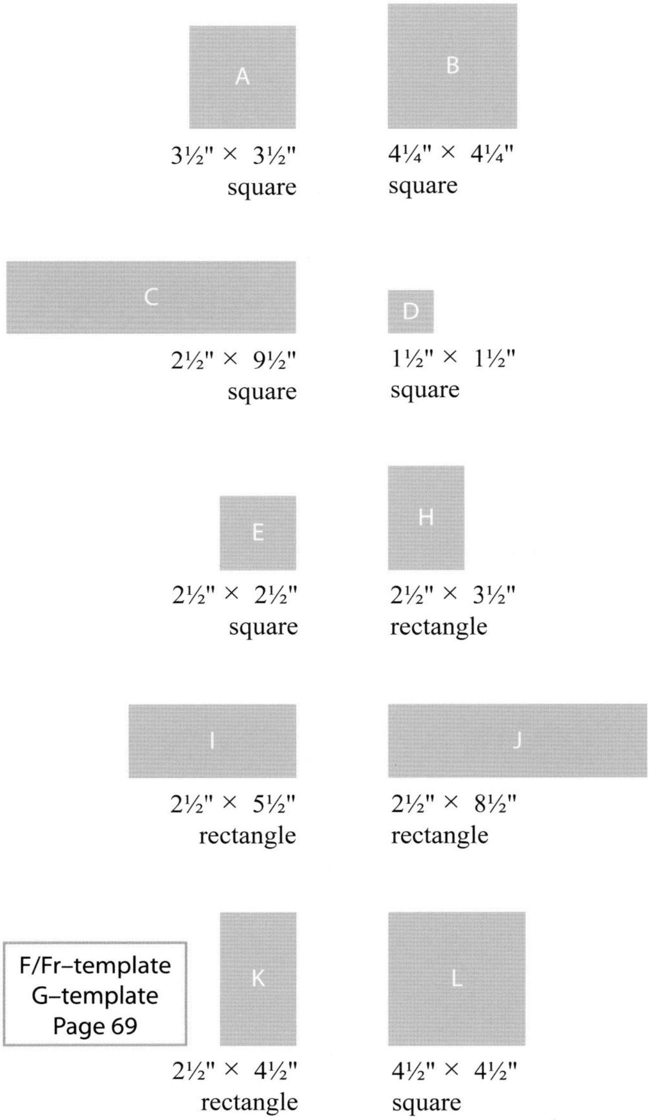

A

3½" × 3½"
square

B

4¼" × 4¼"
square

C

2½" × 9½"
square

D

1½" × 1½"
square

E

2½" × 2½"
square

H

2½" × 3½"
rectangle

I

2½" × 5½"
rectangle

J

2½" × 8½"
rectangle

F/Fr–template
G–template
Page 69

K

2½" × 4½"
rectangle

L

4½" × 4½"
square

CONSTRUCTION TECHNIQUES

Quarter-Square Triangles (page 88)
Flying Geese (page 89)
Corner Squares (page 90)
Border Application (page 91)

ADDITIONAL SUPPLIES

Template plastic

BLOCK CONSTRUCTION

Make 80 quarter-square triangles with the print B and tan B squares (figure 1).

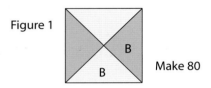

Figure 1

Make 80

Referring to figure 2, assemble the blocks.

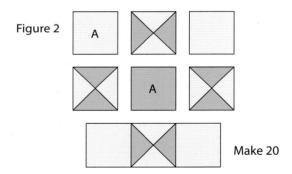

Figure 2

Make 20

SASHING CONSTRUCTION

Using the corner-square method, make 17 sashing units with the tan C rectangles and gold D squares (figure 3).

Make 14 sashing units with the tan C rectangles and gold D and light green D squares (figure 4).

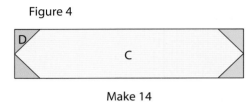

Figure 3

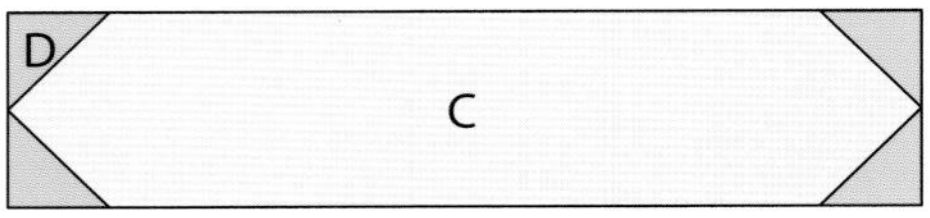

Make 17

Figure 4

Make 14

Make four sashing rows with the sashing units and gold A squares (figure 5).

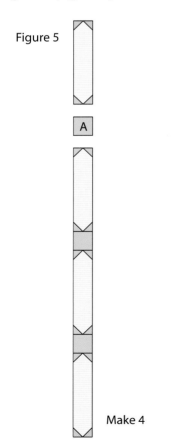

Figure 5

A

Make 4

Join the blocks and the remaining sashing units into rows and join them with the sashing rows (figure 6).

Figure 6

BORDER CONSTRUCTION

Trace the F and G templates on template plastic and cut out on the drawn line (page 69). Cut 18 each F and F reverse from the 2¼" light green strips and 18 G from the 2¾" tan strips (Fr) (figure 7).

Figure 7

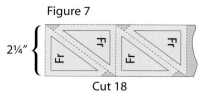

2¼" { Cut 18

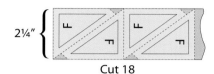

2¼" { Cut 18

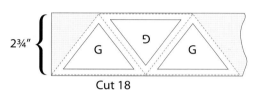

2¾" { Cut 18

Join the F, F reverse, and G pieces to form the border 1 units (figure 8).

Figure 8

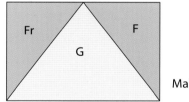

Make 18

A paper-piecing template is provided at the end of this pattern if you prefer that technique to using templates (page 69). You may need more yardage if you paper piece these units.

Join the border 1 units with the H, I, and J
rectangles to make the border 1 strips (figure 9).

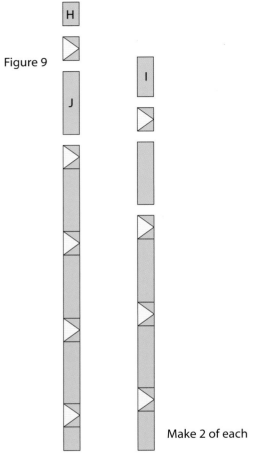

Figure 9

Make 2 of each

Refer to figure 10 for the orientation of the flying-geese units
and add border 1 to the quilt.

For the light green border 2, add the 3½" strips to the sides of
the quilt, then add the 4" strips to the top and bottom (figure 10).

Figure 10

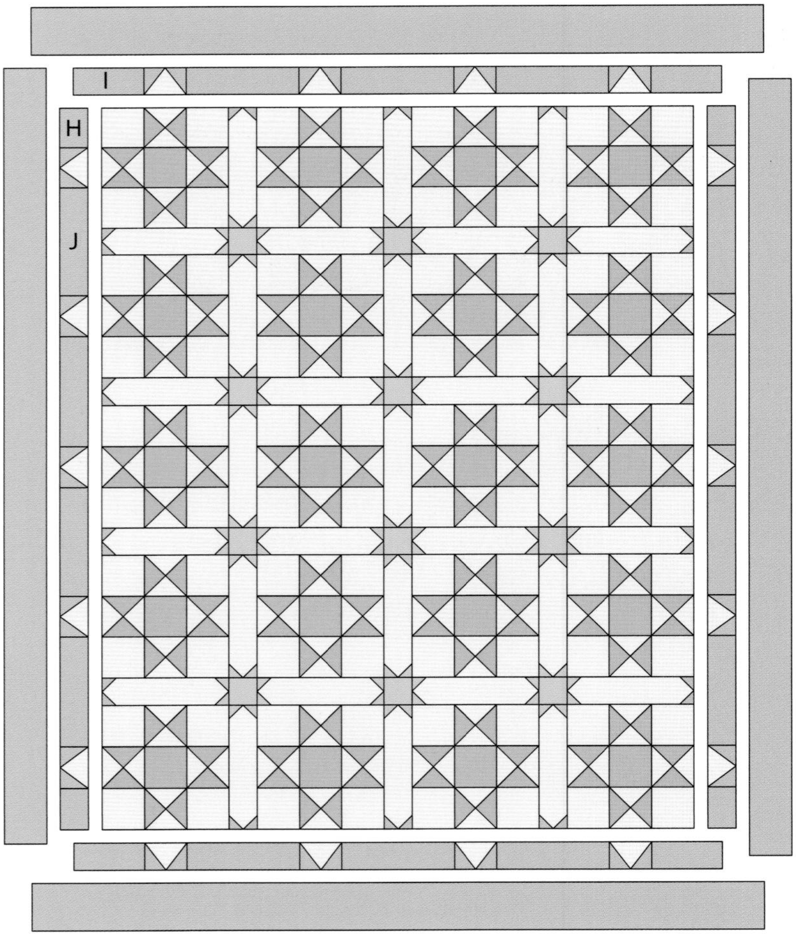

The quilt needs to measure 52½ x 64 for the pieced border 3 to fit. If needed, trim to size.

Make 58 of each flying-geese unit with the K rectangles and E squares (figure 11).

Figure 11

Make 58   Make 58

Join the flying-geese units to make 58 border 3 units (figure 12).

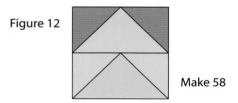

Figure 12

Make 58

Make four corner-square units with the dark green L and gold E squares (figure 13).

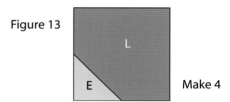

Figure 13

Make 4

Join 16 flying-geese units for the border 3 sides and 13 flying-geese units and the corner-square units for the top and bottom borders (figure 14).

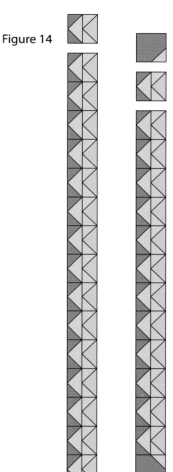

Figure 14

Make 2 of each

Refer to figure 15 for the orientation of the border 3 units and add them to the quilt. Add the dark green border 4 to complete the quilt top (figure 15).

FINISHING

Layer and quilt as desired. Bind with double-fold, straight-grain binding and label your quilt.

Figure 15

PAPER-PIECING & FOUNDATION TEMPLATES FOR BORDER 1 UNITS

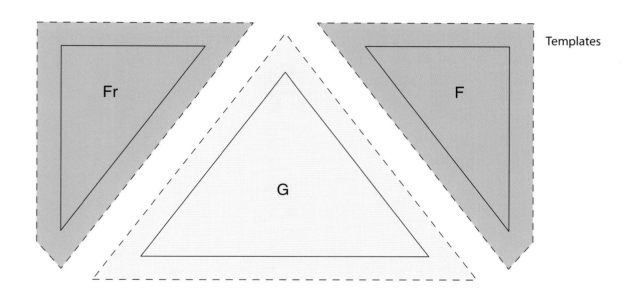

Templates

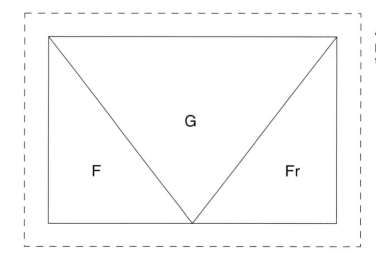

Alternate
paper-piecing
template

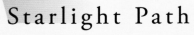

Starlight Path

Quilt size: 81" x 103"
Finished block size: 9" x 9"

Pieced and quilted by Nancy Miller
of Summerville, South Carolina

FABRIC REQUIREMENTS

Light Blue		5½ yard
Print	★	2⅝ yards
Teal	★	2¾ yards
Binding	★	¾ yard
Backing	★	9⅝ yards
Batting	★	90" × 110"

CUTTING INSTRUCTIONS

Use fabric at least 40" wide.

★ Light Blue — *Cut into:*

2 strips	4¼" wide	18 A
21 strips	3½" wide	224 B
5 strips	4½" wide	10 C, 2 strips for strip piecing
22 strips	2½" wide	58 D (border 1)
8 strips	1½" wide	(strip piecing)
2 strips	6½" wide	2 G, 2 H

★ Print

2 strips	4¼" wide	18 A
13 strips	3½" wide	76 F
6 strips	4½" wide	(strip piecing)
1 strip	6½" wide	4 I

★ Teal

4 strips	4¼" wide	36 A
2 strips	2½" wide	24 E
5 strips	1½" wide	(strip piecing)
17 strips	3½" wide	(borders 2 & 4)

★ Binding	10 strips 2½"
★ Backing	3 panels 30" × 110"
★ Batting	90" × 110"

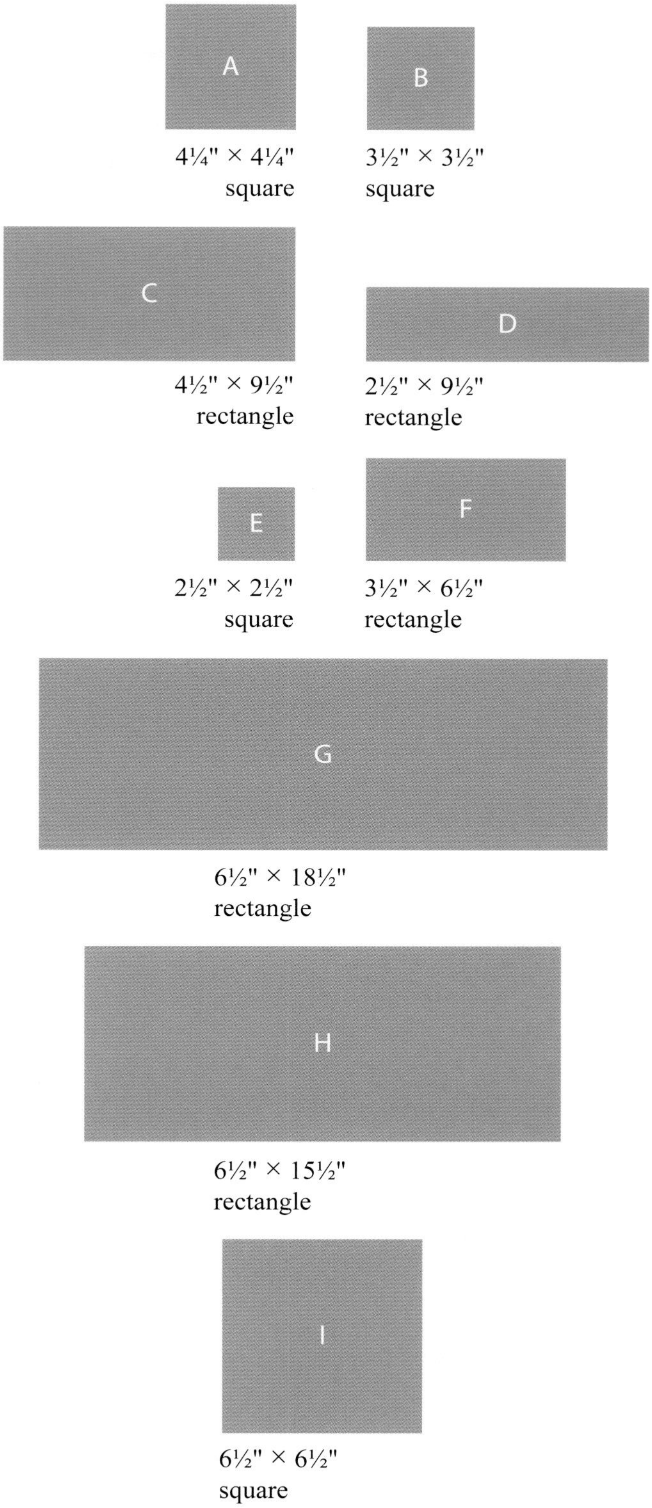

A

4¼" × 4¼" square

B

3½" × 3½" square

C

4½" × 9½" rectangle

D

2½" × 9½" rectangle

E

2½" × 2½" square

F

3½" × 6½" rectangle

G

6½" × 18½" rectangle

H

6½" × 15½" rectangle

I

6½" × 6½" square

CONSTRUCTION TECHNIQUES

Quarter-Square Triangles (page 88)
Flying Geese (page 89)
Border Application (page 91)

BLOCK CONSTRUCTION

Make two strip-sets, each with one teal and two light blue 1½" strips. Cut 36 segments 1½". Make one strip-set with one light blue and two teal 1½" strips. Cut 18 segments 1½".

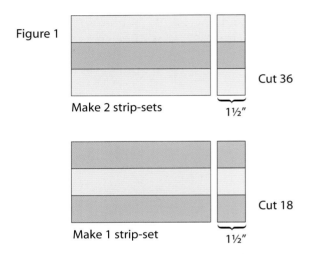

Figure 1

Cut 36

Make 2 strip-sets   1½"

Cut 18

Make 1 strip-set   1½"

Join the segments to form 18 nine-patch units (figure 2).

Figure 2   Make 18

Make 72 quarter-square units as shown in figure 3.

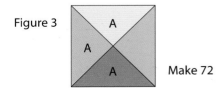

Figure 3   Make 72

Referring to figure 4, assemble 18 block 1.

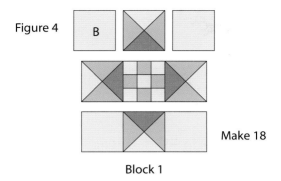

Figure 4

B

Make 18

Block 1

Make three strips-sets, each with one 1½" light blue strip and two 4½" print strips. Cut 24 segments 4½". Make one strip-set with one 1½" teal strip and two 4½" light blue strips. Cut 17 segments 1½" (figure 5).

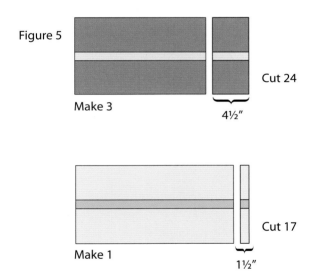

Figure 5

Cut 24

Make 3

4½"

Cut 17

Make 1

1½"

Referring to figure 6, make seven block 2 and 10 block 3.

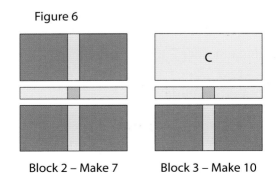

Figure 6

C

Block 2 – Make 7   Block 3 – Make 10

QUILT TOP CONSTRUCTION

Make six sashing rows as shown in figure 7.

Figure 7

Make 6

Referring to figure 8, arrange the blocks in an alternating pattern and join with the sashing strips and sashing rows, placing block 3 along the outside edges as shown.

Make 76 flying-geese units with the print F rectangles and light blue B squares (figure 9).

Figure 8

Figure 9

Make 76

Join 22 flying-geese units and a G rectangle to make two border 3 side units. Join eight flying-geese units, two I squares, and an H rectangle to make the border 3 top. Repeat for the border 3 bottom (figure 10).

Figure 10

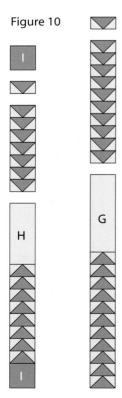

Add the light blue border 1 and teal border 2 to the quilt.

The top needs to measure 63½" x 85½" for the pieced border 3 to fit. If needed, trim to size.

Make 2 of each

Add border 3 to the quilt (figure 11).

Add the teal border 4 to complete the quilt top.

FINISHING:

Layer and quilt as desired. Bind with double-fold, straight-grain binding and label your quilt.

Figure 11

Tic
Tac
Nine

Made and quilted by the author

Quilt size: 71" x 89"
Finished block size: 9" x 9"

CUTTING INSTRUCTIONS
Use fabric at least 40" wide.

☆ Cream	Cut into:
26 strips 1½" wide	68 A, 24 B, 14 strips for strip piecing
12 strips 2½" wide	(strip piecing)

★ Dark Blue

20 strips 1½" wide	(strip piecing)
9 strips 2½" wide	(strip piecing and border 1)
18 strips 3½" wide	46 C, 13 strips for border 1 sides and border 5

★ Gold

21 strips 1½" wide	(strip piecing and borders 2 & 4)

★ Lavender

8 strips 1½" wide	(strip piecing)

★ Green

14 strips 1½" wide	(strip piecing)

★ Light Blue

10 strips 1½" wide	(strip piecing)
12 strips 2½" wide	(strip piecing)

★ Binding	9 strips 2½"
★ Backing	2 panels 40" × 98"
★ Batting	79" × 98"

FABRIC REQUIREMENTS

Cream ☆ 2¼ yards
Dark Blue ★ 3½ yards
Gold ★ 1⅛ yards
Lavender ★ ½ yard
Green ★ ¾ yard
Light Blue ★ 1½ yards
Binding ★ ¾ yard
Backing ★ 5¾ yards
Batting ★ 79" × 98"

A
1 ½" × 3 ½" rectangle

B
1 ½" × 7 ½" rectangle

C
3 ½" × 3 ½" square

BLOCK CONSTRUCTION

Block 1

Make three strip-sets, each with one cream and two lavender 1½" strips. Cut 70 segments 1½" (figure 1).

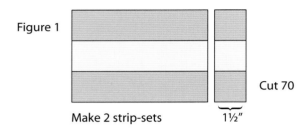

Figure 1

Make 2 strip-sets

1½"

Cut 70

Make two strip-sets, each with one lavender and two cream 1½" strips. Cut 35 segments 1½" (figure 2).

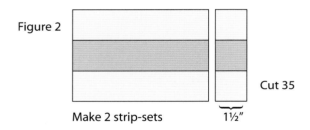

Figure 2

Make 2 strip-sets

1½"

Cut 35

Make 35 nine-patch units (figure 3). Set aside 18 for block 2.

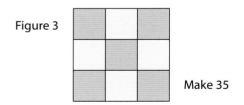

Figure 3

Make 35

Make seven strip-sets, each with one 1½" green strip and one 2½" cream strip. Cut 68 segments 3½" (figure 4).

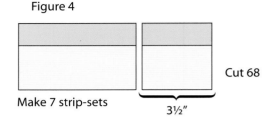

Figure 4

Make 7 strip-sets

3½"

Cut 68

Make six strip-sets, each with one 1½" gold strip and one 2½" dark blue strip. Cut 140 segments 1½" (figure 5). Set aside 72 for block 2.

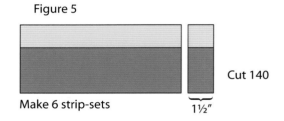

Figure 5

Make 6 strip-sets

1½"

Cut 140

Make five strip-sets, each with one 1½" dark blue strip and one 2½" cream strip. Cut 68 segments 2½" (figure 6).

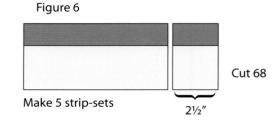

Figure 6

Make 5 strip-sets

2½"

Cut 68

Referring to figure 7, make 17 block 1.

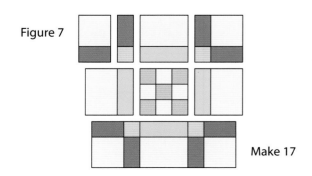

Figure 7

Make 17

Block 2

Make seven strip-sets, each with one 1½" green strip and one 2½" light blue strip. Cut 72 segments 3½" (figure 8).

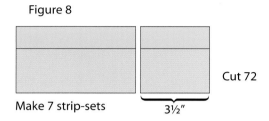

Figure 8

Make 7 strip-sets   Cut 72
3½"

Make five strip-sets, each with one 1½" dark blue and one 2½" light blue strip. Cut 72 segments 2½" (figure 9).

Figure 9

Make 5 strip-sets   Cut 72
2½"

Referring to figure 10, make 18 block 2.

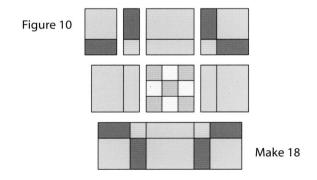

Figure 10

Make 18

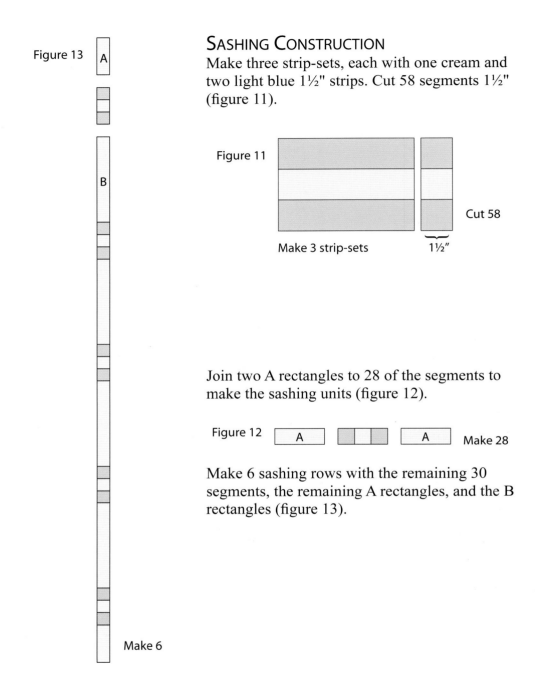

Figure 13

A

B

Make 6

SASHING CONSTRUCTION

Make three strip-sets, each with one cream and two light blue 1½" strips. Cut 58 segments 1½" (figure 11).

Figure 11

Make 3 strip-sets

Cut 58

1½"

Join two A rectangles to 28 of the segments to make the sashing units (figure 12).

Figure 12   A   A   Make 28

Make 6 sashing rows with the remaining 30 segments, the remaining A rectangles, and the B rectangles (figure 13).

Referring to figure 14, join the blocks, sashing units, and sashing rows. Be sure to alternate blocks 1 and 2 as shown.

Figure 14

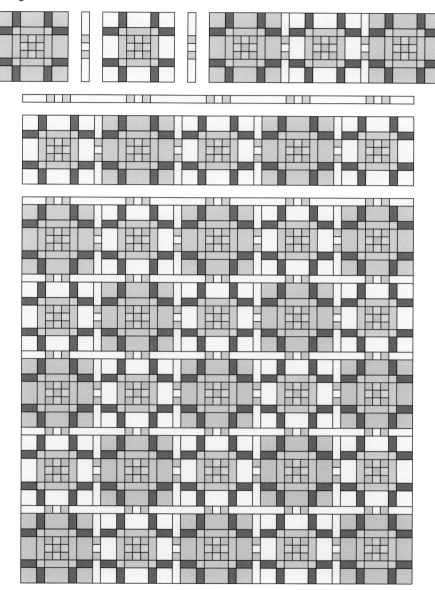

BORDER CONSTRUCTION

For the dark blue border 1, add the 3½" strips to the sides of the quilt, then add the 2½" strips to the top and bottom (see figure 23, page 84).

Add the gold border 2 to the quilt.

The top needs to measure 57½" x 75½" for the pieced border to fit. If needed, trim to size.

Make two strip-sets, each with one light blue and two dark blue 1½" strips. Cut 46 segments 1½" (figure 15).

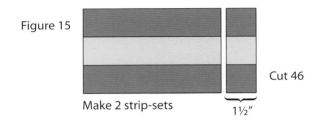

Figure 15

Cut 46

Make 2 strip-sets   1½"

Make one strip-set with one dark blue and two light blue 1½" strips. Cut 23 segments 1½" (figure 16).

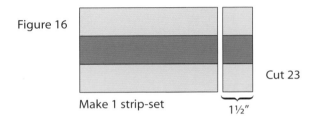

Figure 16

Cut 23

Make 1 strip-set   1½"

Join the segments to make 23 nine-patch D units (figure 17).

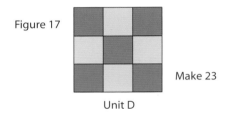

Figure 17

Make 23

Unit D

Make two strip-sets, each with one cream and two dark blue 1½" strips Cut 46 segments 1½" (figure 18).

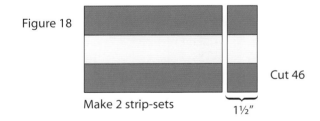

Figure 18

Cut 46

Make 2 strip-sets   1½"

Make one strip-set with one dark blue and two cream 1½" strips Cut 23 segments 1½" (figure 19).

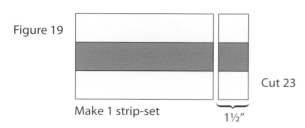

Figure 19

Make 1 strip-set

Cut 23

1½"

Join the segments to make 23 nine-patch E units (figure 20).

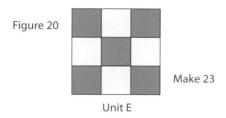

Figure 20

Make 23

Unit E

For each side border 3, alternate 12 C squares with a total of 13 D and E nine-patch units. Begin and end one side with D units and begin and end the other side with E units (figure 21).

Add to the sides of the quilt and press the seam allowances toward the center of the quilt.

For the top and bottom border 3, alternate 11 C squares with a total of 10 D and E nine-patch units, starting and ending with the C squares.

Add to the top and bottom of the quilt, making sure to continue the alternating pattern of D and E units. Press the seam allowances toward the center of the quilt.

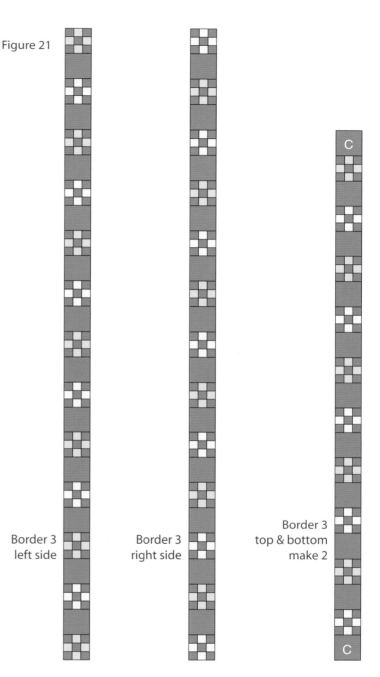

Figure 21

Border 3
left side

Border 3
right side

Border 3
top & bottom
make 2

Add the gold border 4 and dark blue border 5 to complete the quilt top (figure 23).

FINISHING

Layer and quilt as desired. Bind with double-fold, straight-grain binding and label your quilt.

Figure 23

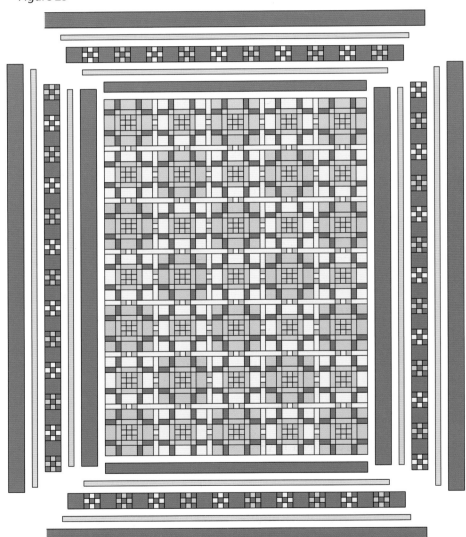

TIPS & BASIC INFORMATION

FABRICS

Use quality fabrics. Quality quilting fabrics can be expensive, but in the long run, because we put so much time and effort into our quilts, skimping on fabric quality should not be an option.

When selecting fabrics, do not stop searching until you find the perfect fabric. There have been times when I knew what I wanted but could not find it, so I used a second (or third) choice. I usually wish I had waited to find the perfect fabric.

PREWASHING

Opinions are split on whether or not to prewash fabric. The main reason for not prewashing is that it takes time and effort. If you have ever had a fabric bleed after a quilt was completed, you probably now prewash every fabric. If a fabric is going to be flimsy and frail after being washed, it is far better to find out before using it in your quilt.

If you do not want to prewash, at least perform a bleed test on fabrics that might be suspect. Submerge a swatch of the fabric in a bowl of warm, soapy water. Allow it to sit for at least 10–12 minutes. If there is any color in the water, the fabric is a bleeder and you will want to choose an alternate fabric or do some further washing or treating of this particular fabric.

If the water is clear, rinse the swatch and lay it on a white paper towel to dry. If the fabric does not bleed onto the paper towel, this is an indication that it will not bleed into the other fabrics in the quilt.

CUTTING FABRICS

Careful cutting of the fabric will help ensure that the blocks and rows fit together as planned. Unless otherwise indicated in the pattern instructions, all strips are cut selvage to selvage.

Fold the fabric lengthwise with selvages together. Manipulate the fabric until the selvages are aligned and the fold line is straight. Lay the folded fabric on your cutting mat.

Figure 1

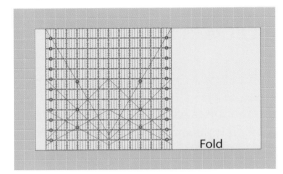

Aligning the fabric

Figure 2

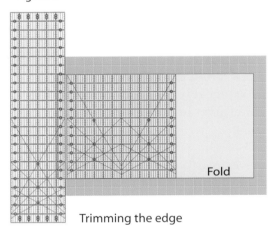

Trimming the edge

Using a large square ruler, line up the bottom edge of the ruler with the fold line, leaving the uneven edges of the fabric exposed (figure 1). Lay a 6½" x 22½" ruler along the left side of the square ruler, covering the fabric edges, remove the square ruler, and cut along the right side of the 6½" x 22½" ruler (figure 2).

After cutting several strips of fabric, you may find that you need to go through the process again of straightening the edge from which you are cutting. By paying careful attention to keeping the fold and selvage straight, keeping the fold and the ruler aligned, and cutting precisely, the strips will be cut perfectly straight. This will help ensure that the quilt pieces fit together.

GENERAL INSTRUCTIONS

Seam Allowances

The instructions for the patterns are based on ¼" seam allowances. Check your seam allowance width to make sure it is accurate.

Pressing

Set the seams by pressing them before they are pressed to one side or the other. Press seam allowances toward the darker fabric unless otherwise indicated in the directions. Be careful when pressing so as not to distort the piece.

Basic Sewing Instructions

There are numerous methods for making any quilt block. The instructions given are based on the following methods. (You may use your own preferred method but be aware that you may need to make adjustments to the yardage amounts given if you do.)

Sewing an Unmarked Diagonal Seam

Align the edge of a rotary ruler with your sewing machine needle and place a strip of masking tape on the machine bed along the ruler's edge as shown (figure 3).

Lay a corner square on the larger square of fabric, right sides together. Sew a diagonal seam by keeping the points of the corner square lined up with the edge of the tape (figure 4).

Trim the seam allowances and press.

Figure 3

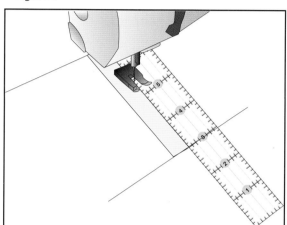

Figure 4

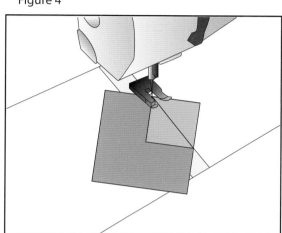

Figure 5

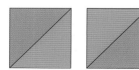

Half-square triangle units

HALF-SQUARE TRIANGLES

Begin with two squares that are ⅞" larger than the finished size of the half-square triangle unit you are making.

Draw a diagonal line across the lighter of the squares. With the two squares right sides together, sew a scant 1/4" on both sides of the drawn line. Cut on the drawn line. Press the seam allowances toward the darker fabric. You now have two half-square triangle units (figure 5).

Figure 6

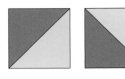

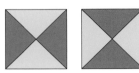

Quarter-square triangle units

QUARTER-SQUARE TRIANGLES

Begin with two squares that are 1¼" larger than the finished size of the quarter-square triangle unit you are making. Make two half-square triangle units as described previously.

Draw a diagonal line across one of the half-square triangle units in the opposite direction of the diagonal seam line.

Lay the half-square triangle with the drawn line over the other half square triangle, right sides together, carefully butting the seam lines against each other.

Sew a scant ¼" on both sides of the drawn line. Cut along the drawn line. Press the seam allowances to one side (figure 6).

Figure 7

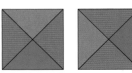

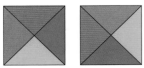

Three- and four-fabric
quarter-square
triangle units

THREE- AND FOUR-FABRIC QUARTER-SQUARE TRIANGLES

To make quarter-square triangle units with more than two different fabrics, first make different sets of half-square triangles. Draw a diagonal line on the wrong side of one half-square triangle in the opposite direction of the diagonal seam line. Pair two different half-square triangle units, carefully butting the seam lines against each other, sew, and cut them apart as previously described, to make the quarter-square triangle units (figure 7).

Figure 8

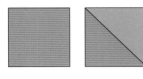

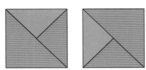

Partial quarter-square triangle

PARTIAL QUARTER-SQUARE TRIANGLES

To make quarter-square triangle units in which three of the quarters are the same fabric, first make half-square triangles with two different fabrics, using squares 1¼" larger than the desired finished size.

Cut a square ⅞" larger than the desired finished size that matches one of the half-square triangle fabrics. Draw a diagonal line across the wrong side of the half-square triangle as shown. Lay it over the square, right sides together, and sew a scant ¼" on each side of the drawn line. Cut along the drawn line. Press away from the quarter squares (figure 8).

Figure 9

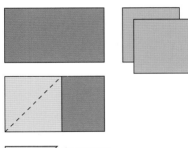

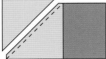

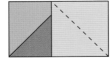

Flying-geese units

FLYING GEESE

Start with a rectangle with a finished size twice as long as it is wide. Cut two squares the same size as the smallest side of the rectangle.

Draw a diagonal line across the wrong side of each square. Lay one square on the end of the rectangle as shown. Sew on the drawn line. Trim the seam allowance, leaving ¼". Flip the triangle up and press.

Lay the second square on the other end of the rectangle as shown. Sew on the drawn line. Trim, leaving a ¼" seam allowance. Flip the triangle up and press (figure 9).

Figure 10

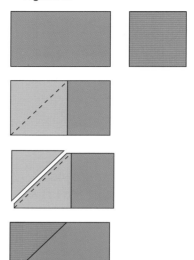

Half flying-geese (or corner-square) unit

HALF FLYING-GEESE OR CORNER-SQUARE METHOD

Use the previous Flying-Geese instructions to add only one square to the rectangle (figure 10).

Figure 11

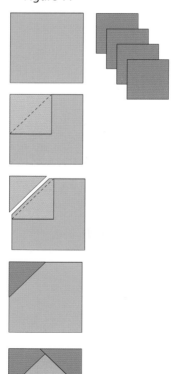

Square-in-a-square

SQUARE-IN-A-SQUARE

Use the previous Flying-Geese instructions to add four squares to the corners of a larger square (figure 11). See the instructions on page 87 (figures 3 and 4) for an alternate method of sewing a diagonal seam without having to draw it.

Figure 12

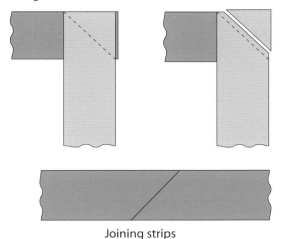

Joining strips

JOINING STRIPS

To make long strips for borders or binding, sew the strips end to end at a 45-degree angle, as follows:

Draw a line at a 45-degree angle across the end of one strip. Lay that over another strip at right angles as shown. Sew on the drawn line. Trim the seam allowances to ¼" and press them open (figure 12).

BORDER APPLICATION

The fabric requirements given for all non-pieced borders do not include sufficient yardage for mitering the corners. If you want to miter the corners, you may need to purchase additional fabric. Side borders are added first, and then the top and bottom borders are added.

MEASURE TWICE BEFORE CUTTING

Before cutting the border strips to the appropriate length, measure your quilt. Measure the left side, the right side, and through the middle of your quilt, top to bottom. These measurements should be the same. If the difference is more than a ½", adjust the seams in those areas that will not affect the points. You do not want to cut off the points of your blocks! Measure again, cut the side borders to size, and sew them to the quilt.

After adding the side borders, measure across the top, bottom, and center of your quilt from side to side, adjust seams as necessary, measure again, and cut the borders to size. Add the top and bottom borders and press the seam allowances as directed. Using a large square ruler, square the corners of your quilt top.

All the patterns call for the side borders to be put on first, followed by the top and bottom borders. Accurate piecing is needed to ensure that pieced borders fit properly. Quilt top dimensions are given at the point where pieced borders are to be added.

FITTING THE BORDER

After working so hard on the quilt top, it can be tempting to slap the border fabric down on top of the edges and begin sewing. It takes only a few minutes extra to be sure your border fits your top, thus avoiding wavy borders.

Fold the edge of the quilt in half by bringing the bottom edge of the quilt to the top edge. Mark this halfway spot with a pin or a chalk marker. Fold again to bring this folded edge (halfway point) to the raw edges, dividing the quilt into quarters. Mark the quarter divisions at the fold lines.

Fold the border strips into quarters and pin them to the quilt top, matching the quarter marks on the border with the quarter marks on the quilt top.

After adding the side borders, press the seam allowances in the directions suggested in each pattern. Square the corners of the borders if necessary, then add the top and bottom borders.

FINISHING THE QUILT

Marking

If your quilt requires marking for quilting, it is easier to mark the quilt before it is sandwiched with the backing and batting. There are many marking tools available, including chalk, water-soluble pens, and pencils. Test your marks on a scrap of fabric to be sure they can be easily removed.

Layering the Quilt

If your quilt is going to be quilted on a longarm machine, there is no need to layer and baste the quilt sandwich. If your quilt is not going to be quilted on a longarm, lay the backing out, wrong side up, on either the floor or a large table. Lay the batting on top of the backing, making sure to smooth the batting and remove any wrinkles or lumps. Lay the top, right side up, over the backing and batting. Pin-baste for machine quilting or baste with a large needle and thread for hand quilting.

★ **LABEL** ★

Documentation of your quilt is important. How many times have you heard questions about when quilts were made and by whom? Do not leave future generations to wonder about your quilt.

Labels can be exquisite or they can be as simple as a piece of muslin on which information is written. Quilt labels should include at least the names of the quiltmaker and the quilter (if different), and where and when the quilt was made. Other information often included is the name of the quilt, the reason or inspiration for the quilt, for whom it was made, and any other information you would like to include.

Figure 13

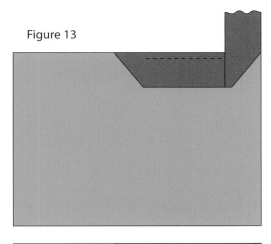

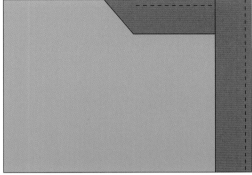

Sewing the corner

Figure 14

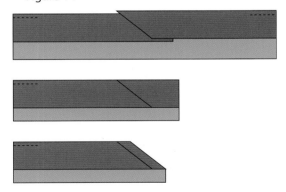

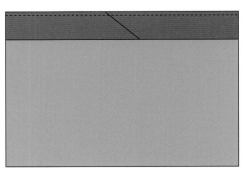

Joining the ends

Quilting

All of the quilts were quilted on a longarm machine. Sources for pantographs and quilting templates are listed in the Resources (page 94).

Binding

Fabric requirements for binding strips are given based on cutting them 2½" wide across the width of the fabric. They are joined end to end at a forty-five degree angle. Trim the seam allowances and press them open. Trim the beginning end of your binding to a forty-five degree angle. Fold the binding strips in half lengthwise, wrong sides together, aligning the raw edges, and press.

A walking foot or even feed foot helps attach the binding smoothly. Begin near the center of the bottom of the quilt and leave a 6"–8" tail free. If using a ¼" seam allowance, stitch to within ¼" of the edge of the quilt. If using a larger seam allowance, stitch to within that same distance from the edge of the quilt. (I use the edge of my walking foot as my guide so my seam allowance is about 3/8".)

With the needle down, turn the quilt ninety degrees and backstitch off the edge. Lift the presser foot and fold the binding back as shown, then fold down along the next edge of the quilt, aligning the fold and raw edge of the binding as shown (figure 13). Lower the presser foot and stitch from that corner to within your seam allowance distance from the next edge. Repeat around the quilt.

To join the ends, leave a tail on the end 6"–8" long so that you now have a 6"–8" tail on each end. Open the folds on both ends so that the binding is a full 2 ½" wide. Lay the ending tail under the beginning tail. (Both ends are wrong side up and lying along the edge of the quilt).Trace the end of the beginning tail onto the ending tail. Add ½" to the ending tail and trim (figure 14).

Join the tails, using a ¼" seam allowance. Press the seam allowances open. Press the binding in half again and complete the stitching. Fold the binding to the back of the quilt and hand stitch in place.

RESOURCES

QUILTING DESIGN PANTOGRAPHS AND TEMPLATES

Willow Leaf Studio
www.willowleafstudio.com

Georgette Dell'Orco
www.quiltersniche.com

Meredith England
www.goldenthreads.com

Circle Lord
Michael & Kay Valeriote
RR 1, 7676 Leslie Rd. W.
Puslinch, ON, Canada
N0B 2J0
www.loriclesquilting.com

RULERS

Creative Grids rulers are available at your independent quilt shops.
www.creativegridsusa.com

MEET JUDY L. LAQUIDARA

In the early 1980s while living in Lake Charles, Louisiana, Judy was wasting time during her lunch hour when she stumbled across a little quilt shop. In the days and weeks following, she spent many lunch hours (and most of her earnings!) in that little quilt shop. She continued to work full time until moving to Kentucky in 1997. From the purchase of a "longarm" machine that was actually a very old, used (very used!) short arm machine, to her present-day APQS Millennium, Judy has found longarm quilting more fun than she ever imagined. "I truly love every minute I spend at the machine."

Designing her own quilts led to requests from friends for the patterns and thus a new business of pattern designs was formed. Several of her patterns have been published.

Judy's quilts have won numerous awards and have been included in books by Bonnie Browning and Karen McTavish.

Judy's photo by Riherd Portrait Design
CATCH A SPINNING STAR by Sherry Rector, Summerville, SC

Today Judy lives in Nevada, Missouri, with her husband, son, and Speck, the best dachshund she's ever had. (He's number 3.) Louisiana will always be "home" and she hopes to move back there some day.

About the Author

Other AQS Books

This is only a small selection of the books available from the American Quilter's Society. AQS books are known worldwide for timely topics, clear writing, beautiful color photos, and accurate illustrations and patterns. The following books are available from your local bookseller, quilt shop, or public library.

#7490   US $22.95

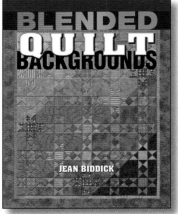

#7078   US $24.95

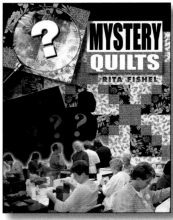

#7079   US $22.95

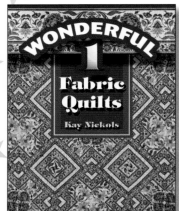

#7487   US $19.95

#7075   US $21.95

#6799   US $22.95

#7491   US $22.95

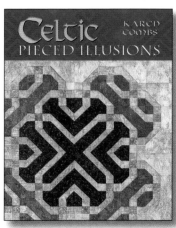

#7014   US $24.95

#6802   US $21.95

Look for these books nationally. **1-800-626-5420**

Call or **Visit** our Web site at **www.AmericanQuilter.com**